IMAGES
of America

ROCHESTER AND
ROCHESTER HILLS

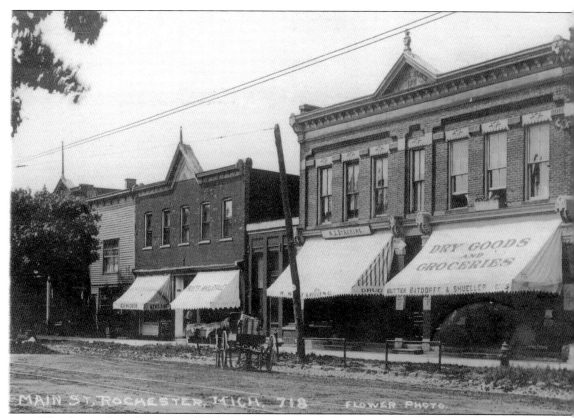

The dry goods and grocery of W.S. Starring, pictured above in 1897, was on Main Street and carried an array of goods including groceries, drugs, stationery, and even wallpaper. During the holidays the store also carried seasonal items.

ON THE COVER: In this photograph are Dan and Jim Williams on the roof of a barn at Great Oaks Farm, where their father was the farm manager. This image exemplifies the spirit of adventure in children growing up in the 1950s in middle-class America. Though the family worked hard, there was still time for fun. The legacy of this farm remains; in 1965, the owner, Howard L. McGregor, donated some of the land to the founders of Crittenton Hospital. (Courtesy of the Williams family.)

IMAGES
of America

ROCHESTER AND ROCHESTER HILLS

Meredith Long and Madelyn Rzadkowolski

ARCADIA
PUBLISHING

Copyright © 2011 by Meredith Long and Madelyn Rzadkowolski
ISBN 978-0-7385-8348-8

Published by Arcadia Publishing
Charleston, South Carolina

Printed in the United States of America

Library of Congress Control Number: 2010934144

For all general information, please contact Arcadia Publishing:
Telephone 843-853-2070
Fax 843-853-0044
E-mail sales@arcadiapublishing.com
For customer service and orders:
Toll-Free 1-888-313-2665

Visit us on the Internet at www.arcadiapublishing.com

To those who dedicate their energy and talents to the perpetuation of history, education, and culture. And to our families for allowing us to be those people.

Contents

Acknowledgments		6
Introduction		7
1.	The Entrepreneurial Spirit	11
2.	Land of Three Rivers	31
3.	Business and Industry	51
4.	Building a Better Tomorrow	75
5.	Men Sturdy as Oaks	109
Bibliography		127

Acknowledgments

We have several people, groups, and businesses that deserve our profuse gratitude. We would like to acknowledge the many historians whose hard work and research came before us, allowing us to give you a more complete and detailed history. Eula Pray, a Rochester teacher, completed her master of art degree in 1944 with her thesis about the history of Avon Township. Wonderfully phrased and researched, her thesis provided us with much of the basic information of this area. In 1969, the Rochester Centennial Commission published a history combining Pray's thesis with fascinating anecdotes from townspeople, some of them the descendants of early settlers. Without this work, the hardships, trials, joys, and laughs of early residents would be lost.

We cannot thank enough those who gave family photographs, time, and assistance to us. Jim Petrucello and the Rochester Hills Library gave complete access to their archives, including the Ray Russell Postcard Collection. Unless otherwise noted, all images were donated by the Rochester Hills Library archives. Patrick McKay and the Rochester Hills Museum at Van Hoosen Farm gave us a lovely tour and photographs. The Oakland County Pioneer and Historical Society proved that a system of dedicated and energetic volunteers can keep a museum going. The Older Persons' Commission hosted open scan days to get personal photographs. We thank the Williams and Snook families for the wonderful family photographs and stories, and as always, the hard work and dedication to history. We thank Larry Stewart at Rochester College, Shirley Paquette at Oakland University, Marlaina Jurco at Avon Players, and Rachelle Kniffen at Leader Dogs for the Blind for their time, enthusiasm, and photographs. Danielle Kaltz from the *Detroit News* and Elizabeth Clemens at the Walter P. Reuther Library helped us obtain archived *Detroit News* photographs. Their images, from the Detroit News Collection, Walter P. Reuther Library at Wayne State Library, have shortened courtesy lines within the text. Larry Baber, Wesley Thompson, Geoff Upward, Alja Kooistra, and Art Snook gave us their time, research, and energy reading our initial drafts. Finally, we thank Meadow Brook Hall, its staff and volunteers, for the encouragement, advice, and access to the Dodge-Wilson archives.

We used multiple sources for our information. When early accounts diverged, we chose the most frequently used report. We encourage our readers to refer to our bibliography for more detailed historical accounts.

INTRODUCTION

Though much has changed in Rochester, many of the same attributes that attracted settlers in the 1820s attract residents today. The proximity to Detroit still allows easy access to goods and entertainment yet Rochester residents remain happy to live in a smaller community. The creeks, once a signal of fertile land and the potential for water power, now mean natural beauty and the potential for recreation. There is no longer the need to cut down the tall oaks to build homes; instead, residents love the shade and privacy they bring to their yards. To the first settlers, these amenities were of course beautiful, but more importantly, they ensured survival and even prosperity.

Records show that James Graham, the founder of Rochester, his wife, daughter, two sons, and their wives reached Detroit in 1813. Behind them was a convoluted journey through a smattering of areas that had proved unacceptable to them: New York, Philadelphia, and Ontario. The passage to Michigan was a difficult one. The Erie Canal was 12 years from completion and the "roads" west were less than ideal for the carts and animals that families like the Grahams towed. Corduroy roads were built along some of the most popular routes; these roads were logs laid horizontally side by side, making swampy or muddy roads somewhat navigable. Even these log roads, which were considered the finest alternative, were expensive to build and bumpy to ride. The unyielding wooden wheels of wagons were much less forgiving than the rubber tires used today, creating bone-wearying travel that many today could not endure—imagine feeling every dip and rise between those logs!

The Grahams treaded new territory for white settlers when they came to Michigan, as there were few formal settlements north of Detroit. Crossing from Canada to Detroit, Graham's grandson William recalled that the whole family perched on a raft while five cows and three pigs swam beside. At this time, many white settlers were slowly encroaching on Native American lands west of the Appalachians just as they had in the previous century on the Eastern seaboard. Treaties and the Indian Removal Acts of the early 19th century did much to damage Indian claims to land. Regardless of the tenuous American–Native American relationship, Graham obtained information from them about the lands north of Detroit that was thick with oak trees, had fertile soil, and had creeks and rivers with enough fall to power mills. This was where his family would settle.

The popular belief at this time was that the land immediately north of Detroit was uninhabitable, which was a response to a public report that stated it was a "low, wet land with a very thick growth of underbrush, intermixed with very bad marshes, the intermediate space between these swamps and lakes is with very few exceptions, a poor, barren, sandy land on which scarcely any vegetation grows, except very small scrubby oaks." Graham was undeterred. It took three weeks for the family to reach Mount Clemens, east of present day Rochester. They followed the Clinton River and several other natural landmarks until finding the juncture of Stoney and Paint Creeks, near where they settled and began to farm. On March 17, 1817, James Graham and his family began the first white settlement in Oakland County when they set up camp; the family is credited with naming Rochester after Graham's wife's hometown in New York. In 1821, the first Rochester school opened in their log house.

The Native Americans who remained in the area and Oakland's white settlers found a way to coexist. Alexander and Benjamin Graham, James' sons, learned the language, allowing them to develop solid relationships. Harvest time was difficult for farmers and for at least a decade there is evidence that Native Americans traveled to Rochester to help during this vital time. Benjamin reciprocated by helping the chief of a local tribe buy supplies to build a house.

Though they were the first to settle the area, the Grahams squatted for five years, allowing a man by the name of John Hersey to become not only the first Oakland County landowner in 1818, but also the first to buy public land in Michigan. Hersey built the first water-powered sawmill in 1819 with the help of Alexander Graham, William Russell, and Benjamin Woodworth. This mill was later converted to also grind wheat flour. This same year, 16 other men bought land in Avon Township. Only 20 years later, in 1837—the year Michigan gained statehood—every piece of property had been sold. Once considered uninhabitable and difficult to access, it is amazing to think that it only took 20 years to disavow this idea.

In 1823, Lemuel Taylor and his family came to Rochester and settled in a valley a mile northeast of Rochester and called it Stoney Creek. The village early on was in many ways considered more successful than Rochester; by 1824, it had a sawmill, gristmill, blacksmith shop, and distillery. Taylor's family were devout Masons and Baptists, and these groups established friendships that bonded the residents together to form a close-knit, relatively self-sustained community. The village they built is still considered to be a fine example of early-19th-century rural development and today contains the Rochester Hills Museum at Van Hoosen Farm. Nathaniel Millerd married Taylor's oldest daughter and ran a general store out of the front room of his house, supplying his neighbors with much-needed supplies from Detroit. He also ran the mail service until Dr. Cyrus Chipman took over. This was in 1824, three years before Rochester's mail service was started. In 1835, the Van Hoosen family emigrated to Stoney Creek where one of the sons, Joshua, started a love story with Lemuel Taylor's granddaughter Sarah Ann. Their second daughter, Dr. Bertha Van Hoosen, became one of the most famous female obstetricians in America, making popular "twilight sleep" during childbirth. Bertha's niece Sarah studied animal husbandry and made Van Hoosen Farm one of the best dairy farms in the nation. Though they were separate villages, the proximity of Rochester and Stoney Creek allowed for a close relationship and an early reliance on each other.

After John Hersey's mill, several others were built to take advantage of the water power in the area. These mills supplied lumber, cloth, grain, and power for all sorts of endeavors. As population grew, so did other businesses: Almon Mack built a general store in 1830, Lemuel Taylor opened a wheelwright shop in 1824, George Shaw made wagons, Hiram Higley tanned hides, and William Burbank opened a furniture factory. As time went on, shops and mills expanded and evolved according to local need.

Schools were built. In 1821, Rochester children began attending school in a log cabin on the Graham property. In Stoney Creek, the children learned from pioneer John Chapman, and in 1848, the village built a one-room schoolhouse. Currently, this schoolhouse acts as a teaching tool, educating local third graders about local history and how pioneer children spent their days. This is an excellent example of the way Rochester and Rochester Hills incorporate the richness of their history into modern times.

Transportation changed the fates of Rochester and Stoney Creek. The first highway, a corduroy road, was built in 1824 from Detroit to Pontiac, with a fork in Royal Oak extending to Rochester. These roads are the still-popular Woodward and Rochester Roads. As mentioned, road transportation was still strenuous and difficult and the Michigan government sought other solutions to connect the state's townships and villages. In 1827, it first tried to reshape the Clinton River into a canal that would potentially connect Mount Clemens with Rochester. When Michigan became a state in 1837, the legislature became more ambitious, attempting to link Lake St. Clair all the way across the state to Lake Michigan; this would have made Michigan a water gateway between the Atlantic and the West. Unfortunately, a multitude of setbacks derailed this grand plan.

Rochester resident and Detroit and Bay City Railroad president Lysander Woodward promoted Rochester as a stop on the north-south railroad in 1871 and Rochester soon had quick and easy access to Detroit, Lake Orion, Bay City, and even Mackinac Island, which changed the potential for production in the small village. In 1869, Michigan Air Line Railroad Company planned to make Rochester a part of its east-west railroad. In 1879, this was accomplished, making Rochester a stop between Port Huron and Jackson. In the 1890s an electric trolley line extended to Rochester from Detroit, once again connecting the residents of Rochester to jobs, supplies, and customers miles away. Stoney Creek, though close to Rochester, suffered when its businesses and townspeople were denied direct access to the railroad; because of this, it never developed the economy of its neighbor.

What had become of the village of Detroit during this time? Its manufacturing might developed through the late nineteenth and early twentieth centuries, creating the industry that would last until the present day: the automobile industry. Instrumental in this world was the work of brothers John and Horace Dodge, who helped Henry Ford with the mechanics of automobile making. Some experts suggest the Dodge brothers' products comprised 60 percent of Ford's finished vehicle. Without their work, Ford might have met another fate. The Dodge brothers ceased manufacturing parts for other auto companies and began their own car company in 1914. Innovations in the field sprouted up everywhere, even in farm towns like Rochester where farmers added a wooden platform to the rear of their cars, inspiring Dodge and Ford to make pickup trucks.

Ford revolutionized the way the world traveled and lived when he offered a generous $5 a day to his workers. Thousands poured into Detroit from the South and from farming communities. As Rochester boys left their family farms for increased pay in "the city," the agrarian town had to reinvent itself to survive. With fewer workers and falling prices for crops, many smaller family-owned farms fell. Some of these farms were bought by "auto baron" John Dodge and later his widow, Matilda Dodge-Wilson. After John Dodge died in 1920, Matilda married a second time, and developed the original Dodge property to some 1,500 acres called Meadow Brook Farms, which she donated to Michigan State University in 1957. Eventually becoming its own entity, Oakland University, as it is now known, was to become one of the only privately founded public universities in the country.

The Wilson farm was not the only large-scale farm to succeed in the area. Ferry-Morse Seed came to Avon Township in 1902, using the fertile soil and easy access to trains to grow the quality seeds it sold across the world. When the business left, Howard McGregor bought much of its property, expanding Great Oaks Farm so his prized Angus cattle would have more land. Another prominent farm was Parke-Davis Pharmaceuticals, opened in 1907. Eula Pray ominously wrote, "No horse or cow admitted to the farm ever leaves it." The company developed vaccines by injecting antigens into animals, and they could not come into contact with the general public once they were infected with a serious disease. Though the process seems harsh now, these animals saved hundreds of thousands of human lives from scarlet fever, tetanus, anthrax, smallpox, and polio, and prevented cattle deaths by blackleg.

From 1915 to 1929, speculators built more than 30 subdivisions in Avon Township. Factories in Detroit and Pontiac required workers, and the immediate suburbs soon filled. Rochester was directly accessed by the Detroit United Railway, passenger and cargo trains, bus lines, and highways, but despite the easy access it was quaint and secluded, a place where workers could escape the city and enjoy their backyards. In 1939, there was another housing boom as automotive factories and Avon Township's National Twist Drill & Tool Co. became epicenters for wartime goods. With the suburban push in the 1960s and the advent of Oakland University and Rochester College, the area saw even greater expansion. In 1984, Avon Township was finally approved as its own city, and Rochester Hills, as it was newly named, became a steady but separate partner from Rochester in the development of the area. Today, with a combined 80,000 residents and a median household income of $72,500, the area is not only considered one of the most beautiful and safe, but also one of the most economically and culturally desirable.

The geography of Rochester and Rochester Hills can be confusing. When the settlements of Rochester and Stoney Creeks were first inhabited, they were nestled in then–Avon Township. The words village, township, and city have specific legal definitions within state government and they change tax rates and definitions by incorporating as a city. This is what occurred within the Township of Avon. In 1869, Rochester was declared a village but was still under Avon Township, paying both village taxes and townships taxes. In 1966, Rochester became its own city within Avon Township, and throughout the 1970s residents made movements to either annex Avon Township within Rochester or make Avon Township into its own city. Most of these attempts failed except in 1974 when 2.2 square miles of Avon Township were incorporated into Rochester. In 1981, however, this was repealed. Finally, in May 1984, Avon Township became a city, with voters deciding the name would be Rochester Hills.

Although it is within the city limits of Rochester Hills, Stoney Creek remains a completely autonomous village and retains the character of the original village. In 1972, the federal government named it a National Historic District, making Stoney Creek a vital part of Avon Township's early history and a way for area residents to step back in time. The Rochester Hills Mayor's Advisory Committee claims it is the "only intact community exhibiting 19th-century development patterns and rural architecture in the area." The village boasts 17 historic structures, including the Van Hoosen Farm, which is now the Rochester Hills Museum.

Though relatively secluded, the Rochester and Rochester Hills region has never lacked a rich cultural and intellectual base. In 1856, Calvin H. Greene wrote to Henry Thoreau praising *Walden* and giving $5 for a copy of his first book, *A Week on the Concord and Merrimack Rivers*, as well as a photograph of the author. Thoreau responded with change, two copies of the book, and the photograph, writing, "I like the name of your county (Oakland). May it grow men as sturdy as its trees. Methinks I hear your flute echo amid the oaks." The daguerreotype of Thoreau was the first one ever taken of him, making it the most expensive photograph to date when it was sold in 1972 for $4,000. It resides in the National Portrait Gallery in Washington, DC. Rochester truly makes "great men" (and women), many of which are featured in this book. With a fabulous library, senior center, Christmas activities, trails, two colleges, and the fourth-largest museum house in the United States, Rochester and Rochester Hills remain diverse and entertaining.

One

The Entrepreneurial Spirit

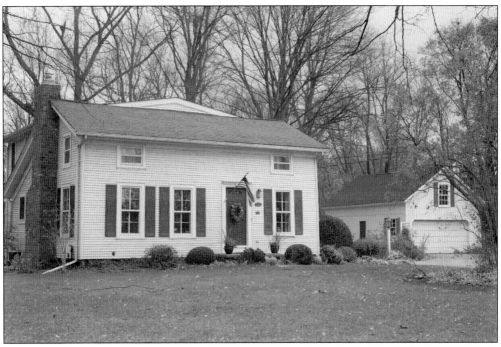

The Ordinance of 1785 helped facilitate the westward expansion of settlements from the East into the Great Lakes region. It allowed for the complete survey and staking of lands in a township and section plan, effectively carving up parcels for sale by the federal government to the public. This influential policy still affects residents' lives; it created the regulated east-west and north-south roads enjoyed today.

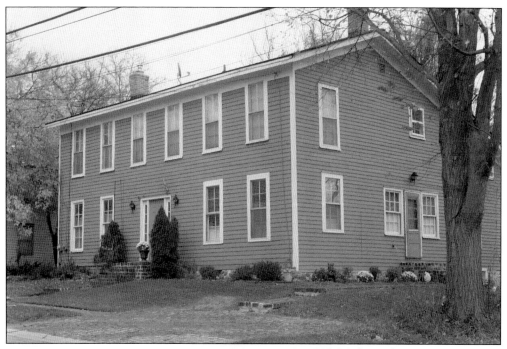

In 1805, Michigan became its own political entity and William Hull was appointed territorial governor, but masses of settlers did not move into the region until decades later. The completion of the Erie Canal made travel from upstate New England easier and more economical. Settlers purchased property from a public land office for less than $2 an acre. Stoney Creek Tavern (above) was built in 1837 and gave travelers a place to rest. (Photographed by the authors.)

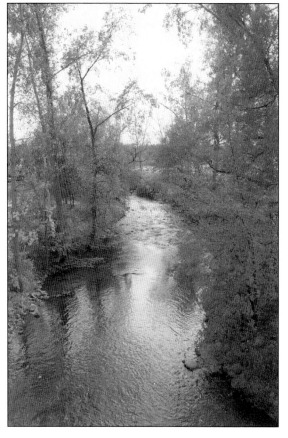

Although John Hersey was the first to buy land in Avon Township, James Graham and his family were the first white settlers in what is today Oakland County. They squatted in Avon Township in 1817, roughly east of Main Street and south of Third Street. (Photographed by the authors.)

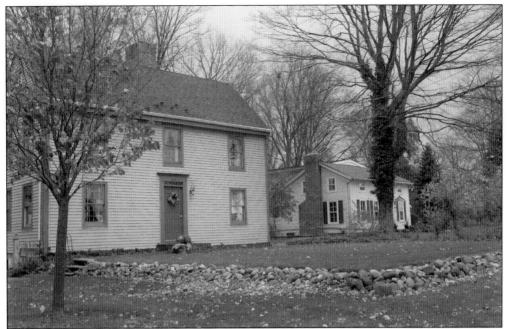

Stoney Creek Village is just northeast of downtown Rochester and is a sister village. The railway chose Rochester for its track and changed the destiny of both small settlements. One of the most intriguing aspects about Stoney Creek is its spelling. The village's name is often found as "Stony Creek" and "Stoney Creek," and the difference has bedeviled the community for more than 150 years. Historians now consider both correct.

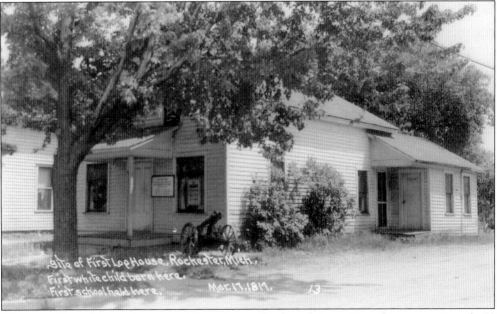

When the first white settlers moved into the newly platted Avon Township, approximately 80 percent of the US population counted farming as its occupation. Land here was abundant and fertile, and within 20 years all the available plots were purchased. This building is on the site of the first log cabin in Avon Township, on Third Street.

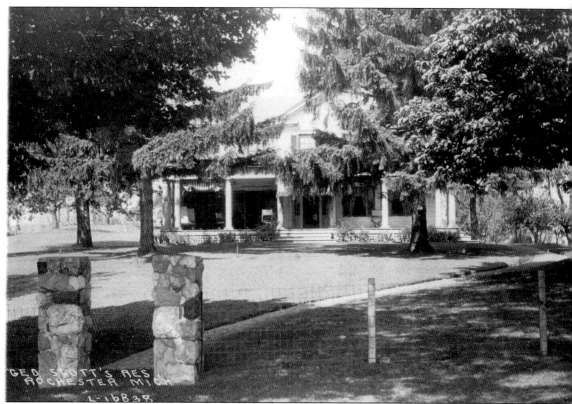

This was the North Main Street home to one of Rochester's most-admired and notable citizens, Lysander Woodward. Farmer, local politician, and businessman, he was well regarded for his role in bringing the first railroad to Rochester. The Detroit and Bay City railroad came through the city in 1872, forever changing the landscape of the agricultural town. This image was captured in 1915 when his daughter was living in the home with her husband. It is a Greek Revival, one of the housing styles to migrate west with New Yorkers to Michigan. A popular style throughout the country from 1825 to 1850, many Americans were sympathetic to Greece during its war for independence (1821–1830) and saw parallels with their country's recent revolution. American (as well as Michigan) city names also showed this influence: Arcadia, Clio, Troy, and Ypsilanti. In 2010, this house was under threat of demolition and redevelopment, but was saved through the hard work of the local historical society.

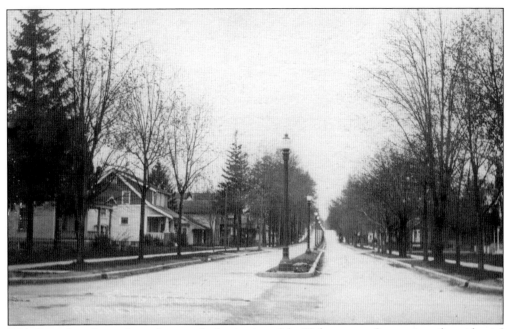

Fifth Street has changed greatly since the beginning of the 20th century. Once primarily residential toward the city center, today it is known as University Drive and is a central business thoroughfare. The Hotel St. James was once on the southwest corner of Main and Fifth Streets. The city was known then, as it is today, for its beautiful tree-lined streets.

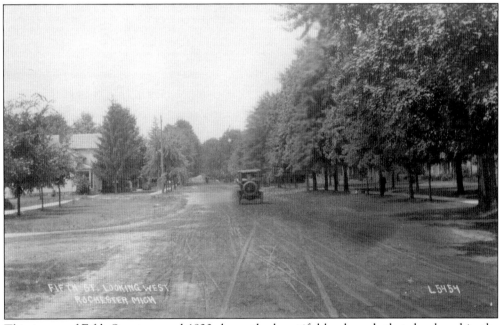

This image of Fifth Street around 1920 shows the beautiful boulevards that developed in the downtown area. Boulevards gained popularity in the 19th century as the City Beautiful Movement—the concept that beautifying urban areas could increase quality of life—took off in cities like Detroit. At one point, Detroit was called the "Paris of the Midwest" because of its many tree-lined streets and boulevards. Smaller towns like Rochester followed suit.

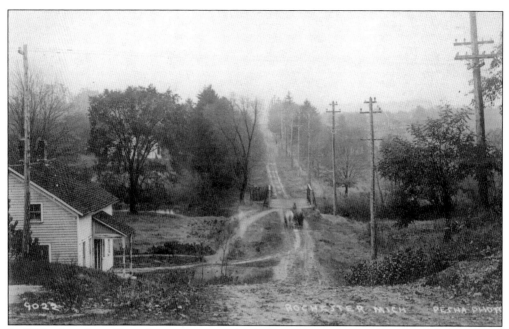

In 1835, when Avon Township was organized, a law was put into effect that required all property owners to serve one day a year working on roads in the area or pay to have someone take their place. The law stood well into the 20th century. Well-maintained local roads were instrumental in creating a healthy commercial region and facilitating community bonds. This image of Main Street looks north toward Paint Creek.

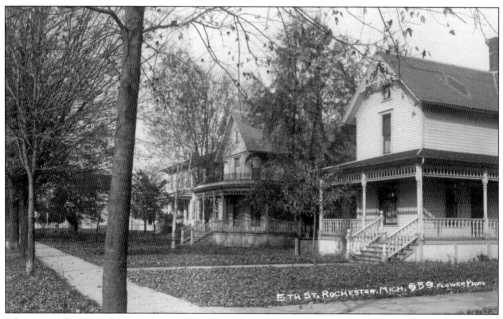

Above is a photograph of two beautiful Queen Anne farm homes on Fifth Street. One characteristic of the Queen Anne style is decorative trim in the gable end of a roofline. Notice the beautiful details on these two homes.

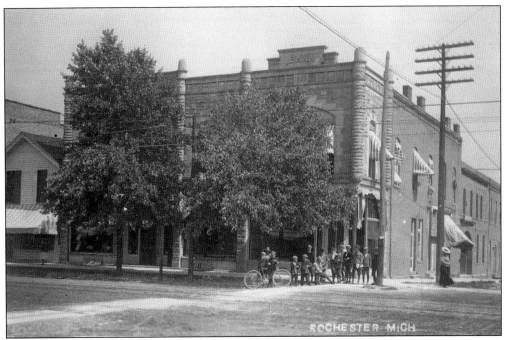

This book seeks to preserve people, places, and stories in historic photographs, but sometimes the story has already been lost. In that instance, the characters are frozen in time and the only option for identification is analyzing the surroundings to try to understand the people in focus. Fourteen young boys hang out on Main Street in front of the Masonic Block around 1920, possibly with a young lady standing in the background. A boy proudly displays what looks to be a new bike to the left of the crowd. Why are these boys on the corner? Why was their picture taken?

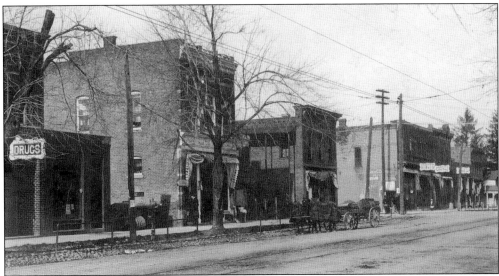

Analyzing old photography is a great way to understand history. Looking at this image, one can see that the trees are bare, so the photograph was taken in winter. The horses pulling the carriage also have on blankets, which demonstrates the way riders protected their animals when it was cold. Old signs, products, clothing, and machinery can all provide an understanding of the time, place, and people in the photograph.

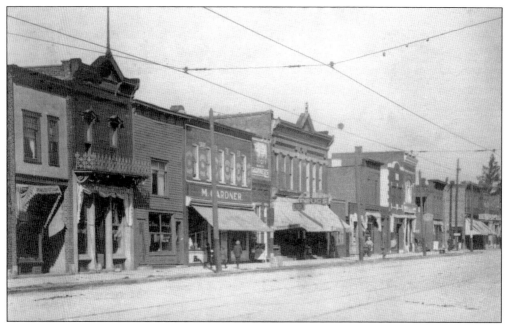

Rochester's beautiful location was a natural hindrance to early transportation. Nestled between hills in a valley, original dirt roads into town needed to be modified to allow for the Detroit United Railway (DUR) tracks to be installed, as the hill coming into town from the south was too steep. This image of 19th-century Main Street shows the interurban tracks running down the road.

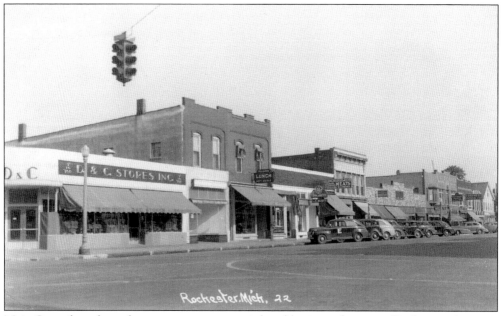

Main Street has always been a strong commercial and business district in Rochester. As many other small towns expanded their business outside city limits to the detriment of healthy city centers, Rochester managed to expand its commercial enterprises geographically while also maintaining a robust downtown. This image from 1946 shows the new kid on the Victorian block, D & C Stores Inc.

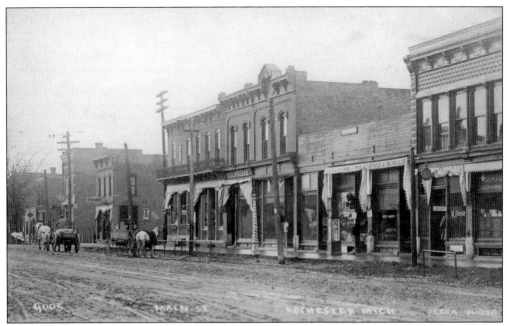

This image shows the many successful businesses in the Palmer block around 1907, including the shoe store of H.H. Stalker. In his day, he was considered one of the finest shoe salesmen in the region and sold many quality brands, including Buster Brown. He also sold caps and hats as well as repaired shoes. Small neighborhood shoe stores are now nearly obsolete in lieu of giant department stores and discount stores.

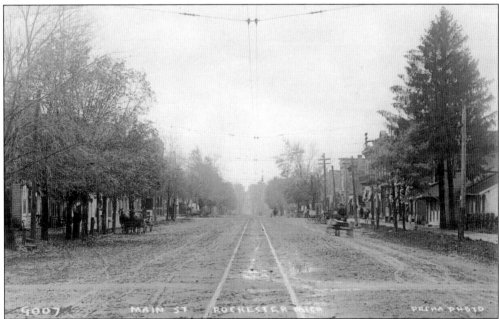

Above is Main Street in downtown Rochester around 1920. Like many downtowns, Main Street was the center of cultural and commercial life for this successful, tight-knit community. The DUR tracks down the center of the road offered the residents of Rochester an ease of transportation not known earlier in the 19th century.

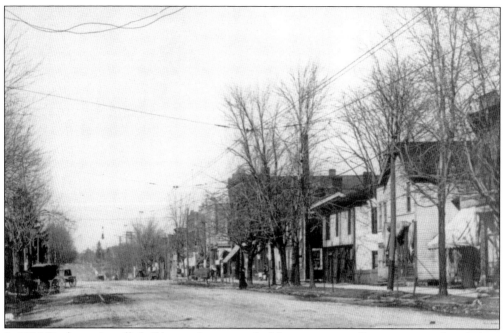

In 1884, Rochester installed oil lamps along several of the main streets. Every evening a lamplighter lit each one with a long torch. Before this time, work and visiting hours were largely restrained to daylight hours. This photograph shows the new electric streetlights installed by Detroit Edison. With electricity, the quality of life inside homes and businesses improved greatly.

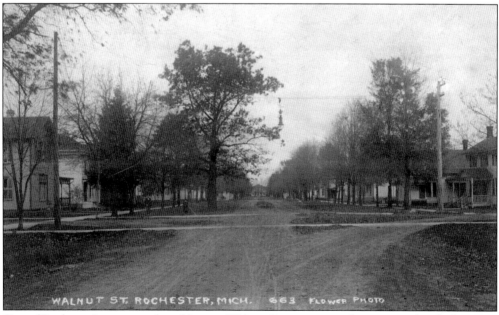

One of Rochester's most popular addresses, Walnut Street, came to be associated with the many churches that dotted its landscape. Later in the century, a boulevard was built down the middle of Walnut Street, only to be taken out again a few decades later to grant better access to on-street parking. The affordability of cars changed the landscape of villages and cities across the country as roads were built and lifestyles adapted to all the automobile had to offer.

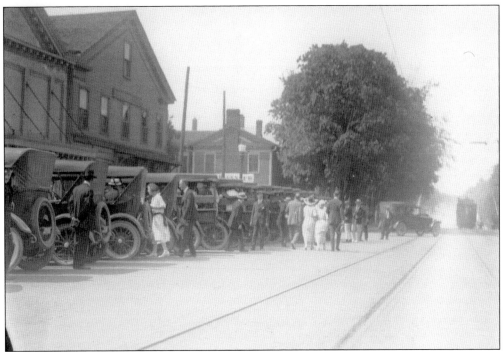

Alfred and Matilda Wilson, the benefactors of Oakland University, were exceedingly philanthropic individuals. They believed it was not what you had, but what you gave that was important, so they gave generously to organizations they loved. Both Presbyterian, they offered their home and grounds to the Detroit Presbyterian Youth to have large annual get-togethers where they could enjoy all the countryside had to offer. Here the youth are making their way from downtown Rochester to Meadow Brook Farms for a picnic.

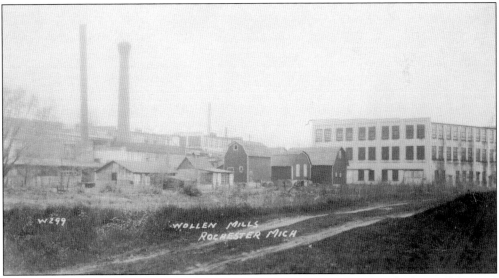

Approximately at Fourth and Water Streets in 1844, Hosea B. Richardson built a mill for wool carding and cloth dressing. Before carding mills, most cloth making was a time-consuming and laborious job for the women of each household. The plant burned later in the century but was rebuilt as the three-story factory seen above, owned by Samuel Richardson, the son of Hosea.

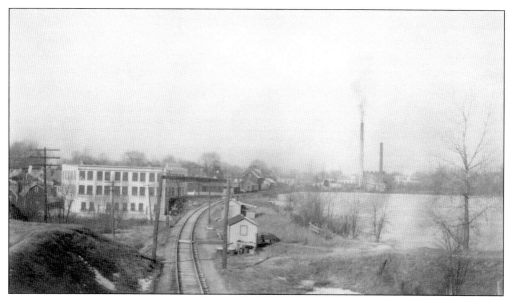

The three rivers in Rochester made for superior industrial operations. Called the Rochester Woolen Mill, this factory manufactured socks and mittens, with most of the wool coming from the sheep of local farmers. This mill burned in 1882 and was replaced in 1897 by a modern building, the Western Knitting Mill, which still stands today. This image shows the close proximity of the railroad, a simple but very advantageous location for any business.

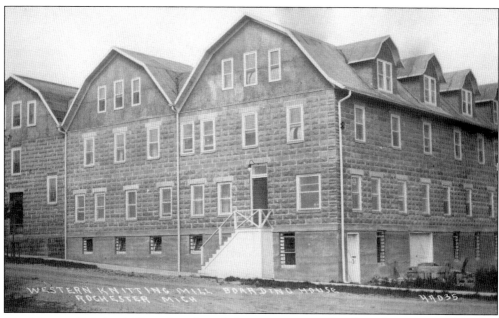

The Western Knitting Mill produced wool gloves, mittens, and socks and was one of the area's largest employers in the early part of the 20th century. The campus had the factory, two warehouses, and dormitories for workers, among other buildings. This photograph shows a close-up of the dorms for single workers. The factory had the capacity for 500 workers. The Chapman brothers, who owned the mills, had trouble keeping employees, who were largely Irish, at the mills until convincing Fr. John Needham to give Catholic masses in town.

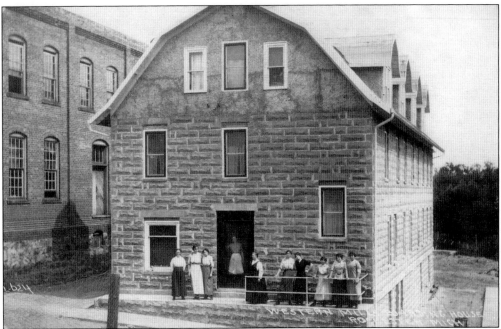

During the 19th century, women began leaving the home and farm to go into the city to work, mirroring the path their fathers and brothers had taken, though not in the same numbers. Society tended to believe that women were naturally better at jobs like textile work because they had been the ones who traditionally sewed and their smaller hands were considered superior for fine work. This image shows the women's housing for the Western Knitting Mill.

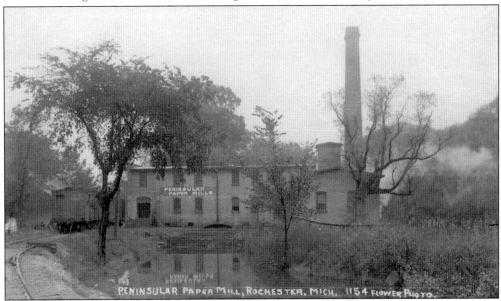

Natural resources were one early reason Michigan gained popularity. Old-growth forests provided the raw materials for many industries thriving in the region in the 19th century, including lumber mills that facilitated the area's physical growth, and paper mills. Paper mills in particular were, and are today, an incredibly odoriferous operation. Locals had to tolerate not only the smoke from industry but also the smells and sometimes toxic by-products that made their way of life possible.

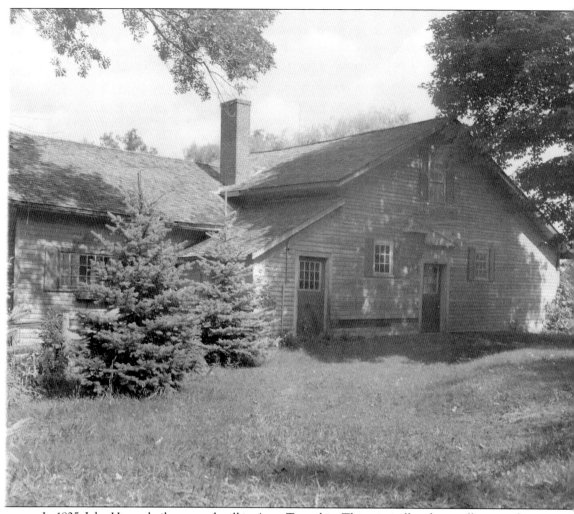

In 1825, John Hersey built a second mill in Avon Township. This gristmill and sawmill operated on his dam near Stoney Creek. In 1868, German-born Joseph Winkler bought the mill and operated it for the next 50 years. He built machinery similar to that used in Germany. Though flour packages called it both "Mt. Vernon Mills" and "Waterville Mills," Winkler's influence inspired its current name, Winkler's Mill. From the end of World War I until 1945, Dorothy Brown used the building as a tearoom and antique shop. Though Winkler's Mill burned in 1985, the houses built around it form a state-designated historical district. In 2010, Mayor Bryan K. Barnett established an advisory committee to establish a plan to both preserve the area and update it to satisfy the needs of area residents. Surrounded by narrow country roads and old oaks, it is a virtual time machine.

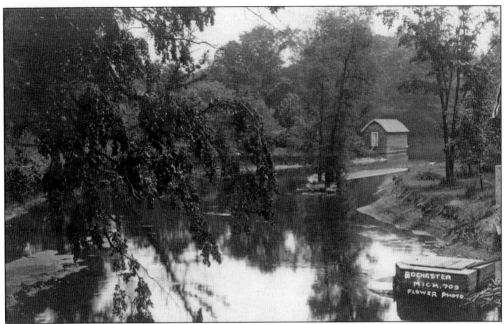

The beauty of Rochester is hard to beat, whether in the 19th century or today. Either natural or man-made, the water and waterways of the area continue to be a dominant factor in Rochester's identity. Water made so much of what was considered Rochester possible. When Western Knitting Mill dammed Paint Creek for a power source, Chapman's Pond, above, resulted. The 12-acre millpond was named after two instrumental partners of the business, the Chapman brothers. On June 18, 1946, Paint Creek spilled over, breaking the McAleer Dam and pushing Chapman's Pond beyond its shores and into the streets of east Rochester, as seen below. A woman on Third Street died while trying to escape. Train tracks, streets, and buildings suffered damage. Since the dam had not been used for power for years, the pond was filled in. Once a popular swimming hole, fishing spot, and center of winter ice sports, Chapman's Pond now exists only in memories. (Bottom photograph courtesy of the Walter P. Reuther Library.)

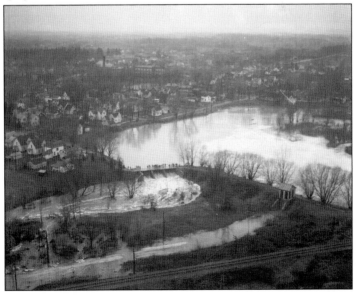

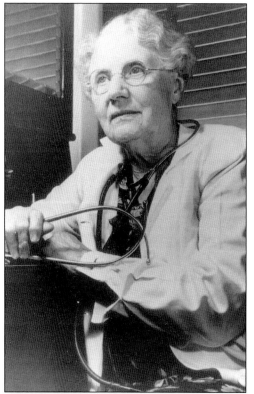

Finding it difficult to work after graduating from the University of Michigan in 1888, Rochester native Dr. Bertha Van Hoosen moved to Chicago. While there, she made house calls, had a clinic in her apartment, and developed several women's clinics and hospitals. She eventually made a name for herself, and the male students who once ridiculed her fought to take her classes. The 1895 photograph below reveals a comfortable hospital room with a nurse, patient, and visitor. Van Hoosen believed her female patients deserved a clean, bright, homey place to recover and worked to bring better hygiene practices to the world of medicine. In 1948, she posed for the iconic photograph at left. By then, she was famous for changing the medical field for female doctors and patients. She pioneered a buttonhole appendectomy and "twilight sleep" for birthing mothers, and she always offered respect and civilized health care for patients, regardless of their station in life. (Courtesy of Rochester Hills Museum.)

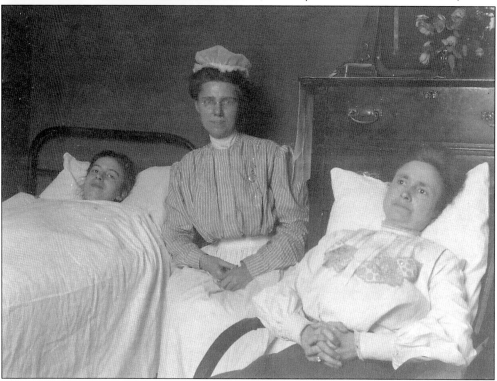

Taken at a studio, this 1890s photograph shows Alice Van Hoosen and three friends posing with traditionally male sporting props. From left to right are Julia ?, Matie Lepham, Alice Van Hoosen, and Carrie Barker holding an oar, a shotgun, and bows. Seven years older than Bertha, Alice taught in Pontiac while Bertha went to high school there. Alice married Joseph Comstock Jones and later accompanied Bertha to medical conferences, sometimes bringing her daughter Sarah. (Courtesy of Rochester Hills Museum.)

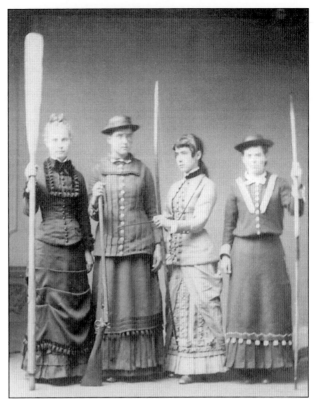

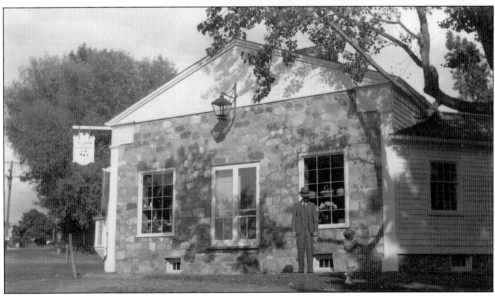

Sarah Van Hoosen Jones sold the milk from her Holstein and Guernsey cattle locally. Her dairy farm was renowned for being clean and producing a high-butterfat milk. In 1941, the Holstein Friesian Association of America tested butterfat and production of several dairy farms, including Sarah's. Her herd averaged 2.5 times higher butterfat. In 1938, she built At the Sign of the Black and White Cow, which sold her products as well as homemade goods from local housewives. (Courtesy of Rochester Hills Museum.)

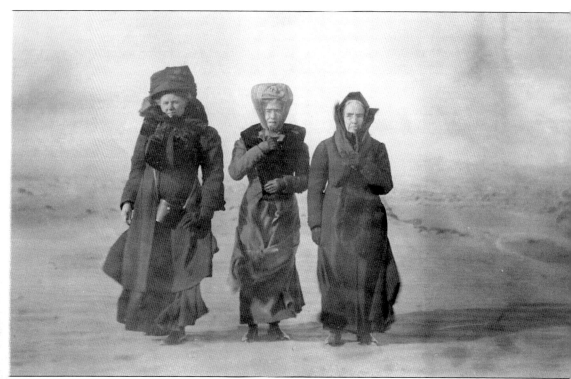

Dr. Bertha Van Hoosen enlightened her rural family by exposing them to a world previously unknown, taking them on trips to Europe, Asia, and Africa. Pictured in 1910, from left to right, are Bertha, Alice, and their mother, Sarah Van Hoosen, in the Sahara Desert. Alice's daughter Sarah's ill health kept her from social pursuits so it was decided a year abroad would prepare her for college. The family travelled with Bertha for her lecture at the 16th International Medical Congress in Budapest. Bertha's account of this year attending foreign clinics gives a detailed account of current medical practices. In *Petticoat Surgeon*, she wrote of the hygiene, manner of dress, surgical techniques, and other customs of doctors and surgeons in other countries. While abroad, she was questioned about her friend, the legendary surgeon and founder of the Mayo Clinic, Dr. William Worrall Mayo's hygiene! In Algiers, one of their favorite stops on the tour, they visited the Sahara Desert. (Courtesy of Rochester Hills Museum.)

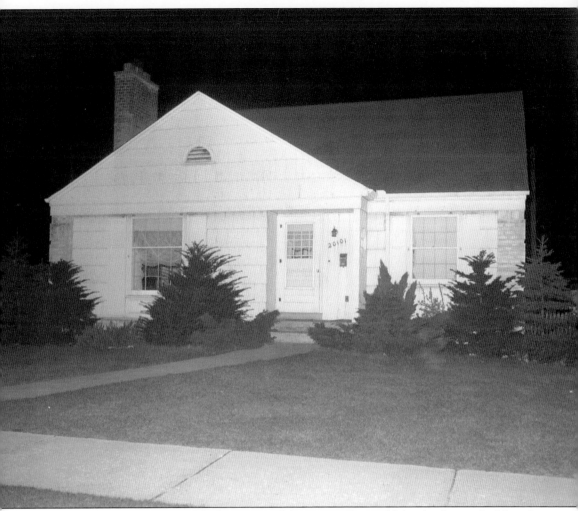

Walter P. Reuther is renowned for being one of the most influential labor leaders in the United States. From 1950 to 1970, he and his family lived in this house with posted guards, keeping them far away from those who sought to harm him. Simultaneously loved and despised depending on your stance on labor rights, this West Virginia–bred man, who was laid off by Ford during the Great Depression, took the automotive hub of Detroit by storm when he asked for fair treatment and better pay for factory workers. He was president of the United Automobile Workers of America and was famously called "the most dangerous man in Detroit" for organizing strikes, uniting factory workers against a common cause, and gaining public attention for his work. Also a supporter of African American civil rights, he stood beside Martin Luther King Jr. when he gave his "I Have A Dream" speech in Washington, DC on August 28, 1963. (Courtesy of the Walter P. Reuther Library.)

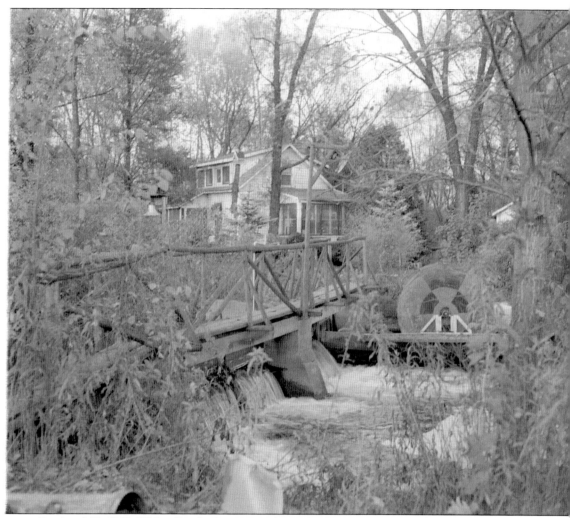

On April 20, 1948, Walter Reuther's arm was shot at his Detroit apartment; he was almost killed. A year later, his brother Victor's eye was shot out. Reuther had already endured two assassination attempts, a kidnapping attempt, several beatings, and enough vitriolic and hateful comments to make any man hide, but it was the concern for his family after his brother's injury that led him to take extra precautions. In 1950, he and his family moved to Oakland Township/Rochester in this home along Paint Creek. It was a tiny summer cottage, but, partly for pleasure and partly for therapy for his injured arm, Reuther rebuilt it by hand. His family loved living in the country and they were much involved in conservation efforts for Paint Creek. It is obvious from this photograph that they enjoyed maintaining their picturesque backyard. In 1970, Walter and his wife, May, died in a private plane accident. (Courtesy of the Walter P. Reuther Library.)

Two
LAND OF THREE RIVERS

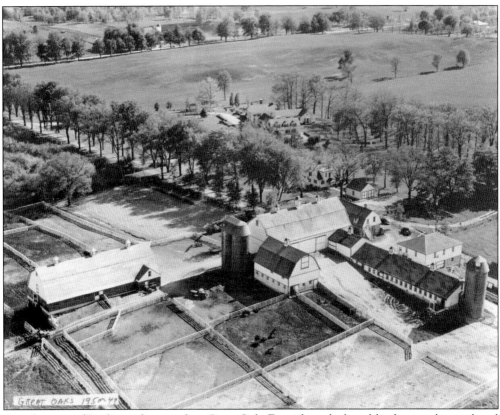

Aerial images of Rochester farms such as Great Oaks Farm show the breadth of regional agricultural operations and how much the landscape has really changed from the way it once looked. As suburbanization and industrialization transformed areas such as Rochester, these farms slowly became cherished memories. (Courtesy of the Williams family.)

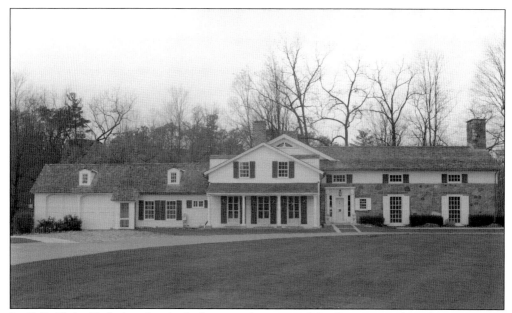

In 1840, Elisha Taylor's widow built the central portion of this house to replace the original log cabin. In 1863, Joshua Van Hoosen bought his mother-in-law's house and took over the Taylor farm. In the 1920s, Bertha, Sarah, and Alice moved the farmhouse and added wings. As they travelled the world they gathered souvenirs that are now on display in this museum. (Photographed by the authors.)

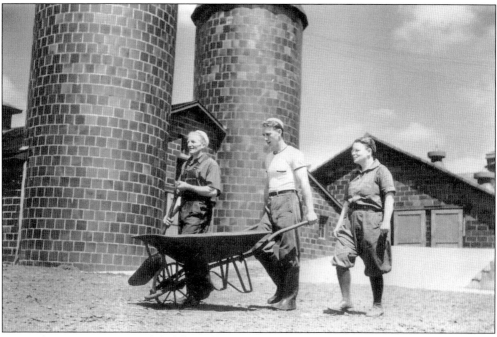

Dr. Sarah Van Hoosen Jones, left, followed her grandfather Joshua Van Hoosen's example by taking over the family farm after earning a master's degree in animal husbandry and a doctorate degree in animal genetics. She expanded the farm by adding several outbuildings and these silos. They now house part of the Rochester Hills Museum. (Courtesy of Rochester Hills Museum.)

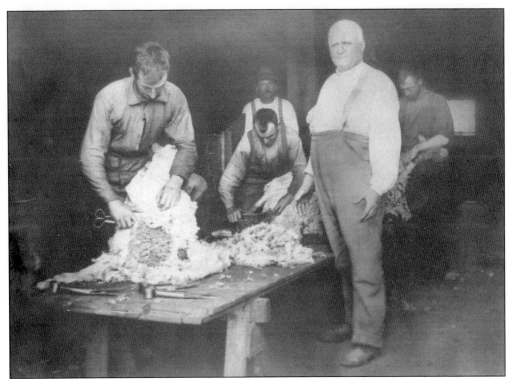

Dr. Bertha Van Hoosen took this photograph of, from left to right, Chas Tyrell, unidentified, Joe Young, her father Joshua, and unidentified around 1890. Bertha wrote fondly in *Petticoat Surgeon* of watching her father shear sheep every spring, recalling the warm soft wool and newly shorn sheep that became barely recognizable to their lambs. (Courtesy of Rochester Hills Museum.)

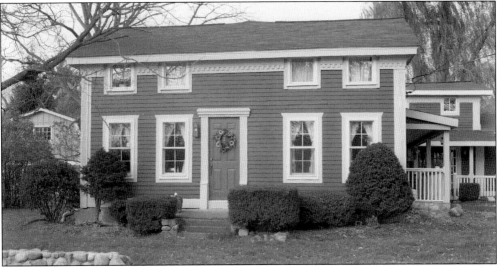

Although the Van Hoosen farmhouse is immortalized for the work Bertha and her niece Sarah did, it was actually Bertha's grandmother Mary Taylor's house. Bertha and Alice were born in the house above, an 1835 Stoney Creek farmhouse owned by Joshua Van Hoosen. Modern additions have been added to the rear of the house, but like the rest of Stoney Creek, the genuine character of it has been preserved. (Photographed by the authors.)

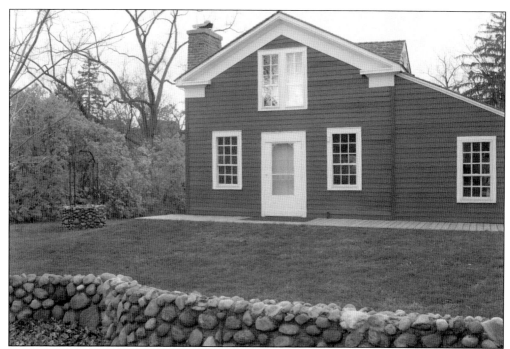

The Rochester Hills Museum at Van Hoosen Farm uses this 1850 Greek Revival house to show what home life was like for farm laborers. Sarah Van Hoosen bought it to house the tenants she hired to help her on her dairy farm. Additions have been made to the house twice, ostensibly to service a larger family. In 1955, she famously painted it red to match a similar home she saw in Vermont. Notice the stone well at the left side. (Photographed by the authors.)

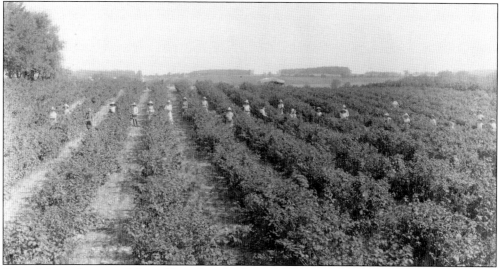

One of the cash crops of Avon Township was berries. This c. 1900 photograph shows the A.L. Ross Farm at the southeast corner of Tienken and Brewster Roads. Between every row of bushes, a worker stands with a wide-brimmed hat and wooden box strung around his neck. Berry farmers loaded the short-lived berries onto the Michigan Central Train to go to Detroit. Once backbreaking work, berry farms in Oakland County are now a source of recreation. (Courtesy of Rochester Hills Museum.)

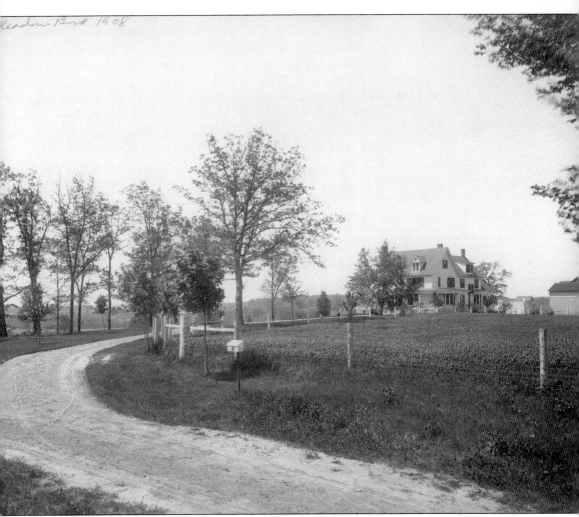

In 1908, automobile baron John Dodge and his third wife, Matilda Rausch Dodge, lived in Detroit but explored Avon Township looking for a property to use as their weekend retreat. Detroit was a busy industrial town at the time and those who could afford to find a place in the country, did. Lore has it that upon seeing Mr. Higgins's farm on Adams Road, John and Matilda fell in love and immediately offered to buy it. The gentleman, not looking to sell and not knowing who stood in front of him, said that it was not for sale. Not to be discouraged, John said "How much?" to which Higgins quoted an exorbitant price, thinking this man would be shocked and politely excuse himself and leave. But instead, John took out his checkbook and wrote him a check! This home, with many subsequent additions, can still be seen just north of Avon Road on the campus of Oakland University. (Courtesy of Meadow Brook Hall.)

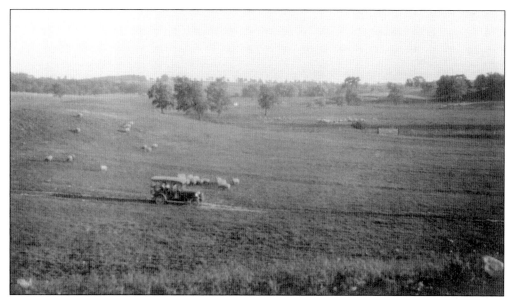

A photograph from around 1908 shows the land surrounding Meadow Brook Farms. At this time, John and his brother Horace were quickly making a name for themselves in Detroit designing and producing automobile components for local car companies. This car foreshadows the automobile's ability to bring the country closer and to allow city residents to move to outlying areas and commute to work. (Courtesy of Meadow Brook Hall.)

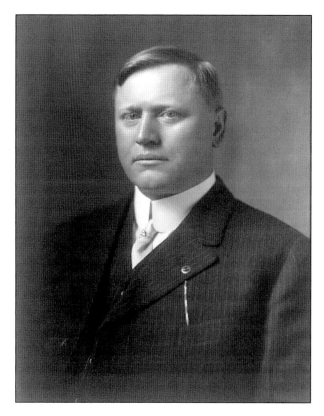

At left is a portrait of John Dodge. Together with his brother Horace, he created the Dodge Brothers Motor Car Company. Starting out fabricating parts for other car companies, some sources claim that by 1913 an estimated 60 percent of a Ford car was actually made of Dodge parts. By 1914, the brothers had decided to manufacture their own vehicles. Both sporty and luxurious, the cars quickly became popular. (Courtesy of Meadow Brook Hall.)

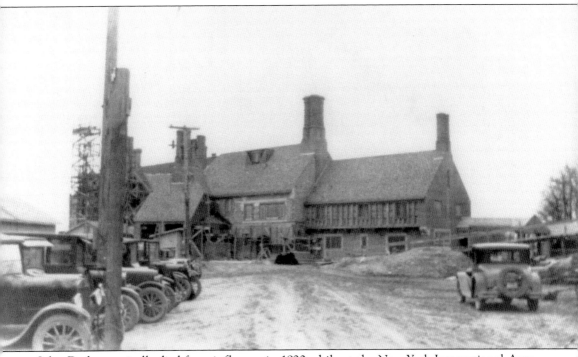

John Dodge tragically died from influenza in 1920 while at the New York International Auto Show, leaving his widow, Matilda, and three small children, Frances, Daniel, and Anna Margaret. John's brother Horace died later that same year. For five years Matilda mourned John's death, then met an eligible Presbyterian bachelor from her church and fell in love. She married Alfred Wilson, who had a lumber business and was living in Detroit at the time, although he was originally from Wisconsin. The two of them decided to take the Dodge country property and build the spectacular Meadow Brook Hall between 1926 and 1929, seen here under construction. The Wilsons were fastidious collectors of all things related to their home, and the Meadow Brook Hall archives house a wonderful collection of construction photographs from the farm and hall. (Courtesy of Meadow Brook Hall.)

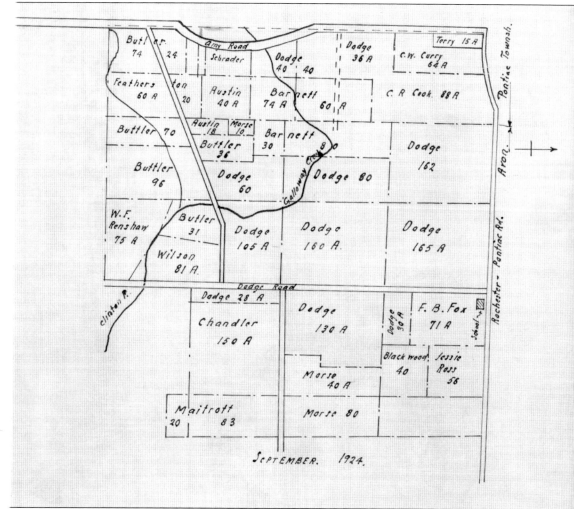

Meadow Brook Hall is considered the premier example of English Revival architecture in the country. It was completed at a cost of $4 million, an amount that would be, by some estimates, $80 to $120 million today. For Alfred and Matilda Wilson, it was the crowning jewel to their farm property that would grow to be 1,500 self-sufficient acres from the 350 acres John Dodge originally developed, seen on this map. It would contain award-winning stables for both American Saddlebred (developed by Matilda's daughter Frances Dodge Van Lennep) and Belgian horses bred by Matilda Wilson. (Courtesy of Meadow Brook Hall.)

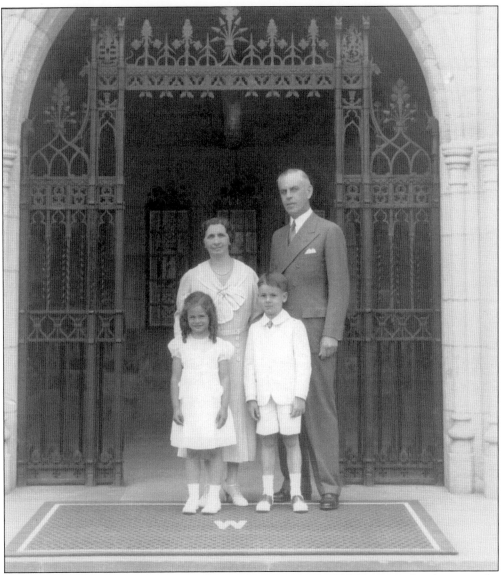

When Meadow Brook Hall was complete, it was a staggering 88,000-square-foot home in the English Revival style. The Wilsons moved in with Frances and Daniel (Anna Margaret had passed away at age four), and they adopted two children: Richard in 1930 and Barbara in 1931. They are seen here at the front entrance of Meadow Brook. The six of them lived in the house with a full staff that at times numbered 28 people. (Courtesy of Meadow Brook Hall.)

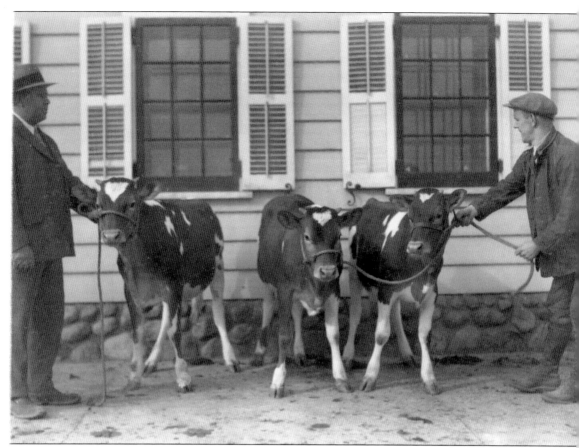

The Wilsons were very proud of the self-sufficiency of their farm. Wealthy enough to be "gentlemen farmers" who took a hands-off approach to their business, the Wilsons believed if something was worth doing, it was worth doing right, so they actively managed the day-to-day operations, each overseeing a different area. The farm raised Hereford cattle, Guernsey cows, poultry, pigs, and horses. Above is farm manager John Cline with Frank Gay, a dairy herdsman. Frank Gay's daughter Barbara Gay Thorpe grew up on Meadow Brook Farms and dedicated much of her adult life to volunteering once the Hall opened as a museum in 1971. Guests touring the Hall would often hear stories of how much she enjoyed her childhood on the estate. She passed away in 2009. (Courtesy of Meadow Brook Hall.)

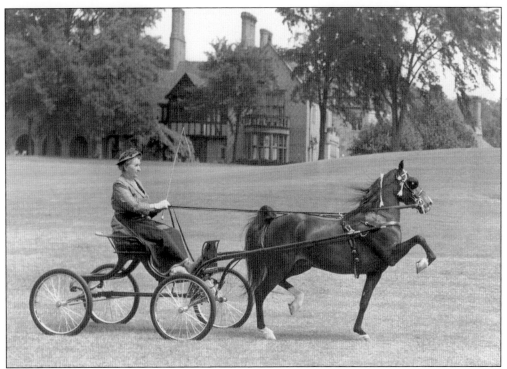

Matilda managed one of the more high-profile farm groups, the Belgian draft horses. Strong-willed and independent, this diminutive woman was often seen working directly with them, despite her 5-foot, 2-inch frame. Showing their horses regionally as well as nationally, she was often the first place winner and many times beat her rival, the Budweiser hitch. She also had Hackney ponies, seen here. (Courtesy of Oakland University.)

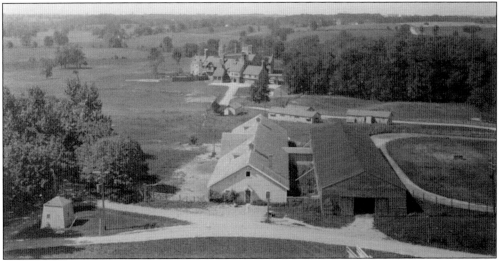

Dodge Stables was built at Meadow Brook Farms in 1935. As it grew, it eventually boasted one of the largest indoor riding arenas in the country. Frances Dodge, the daughter of Matilda and her first husband, John, founded the famed stables from this location and developed it into an award-winning breeding program for both Hackney ponies and American Saddlebred horses before moving the operation to Castleton Farms in Kentucky. (Courtesy of Meadow Brook Hall.)

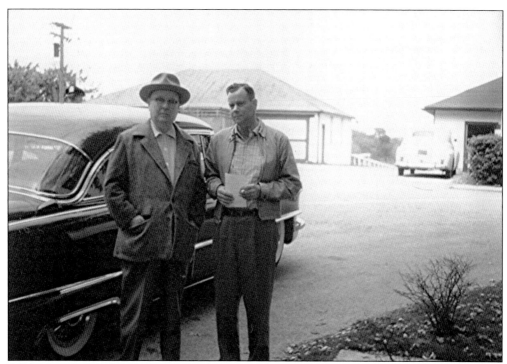

Of the many great farms in Avon Township, Great Oaks Stock Farm lives on in the hearts of Rochester residents because of the McGregor family's gift of part of their farm for the creation of Crittenton Hospital, built in 1967. This image shows Howard McGregor Sr. and farm manager Robert Williams in 1958. Registered Aberdeen Angus cattle were bred at Great Oaks Stock Farm. (Courtesy of the Williams family.)

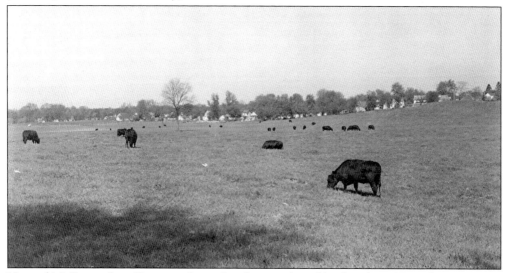

Howard McGregor Sr., a Detroit industrialist, first purchased land in Avon Township in 1938 to breed purebred cattle and to own a piece of land in the country for his family to enjoy. Great Oaks Stock Farm accomplished both. McGregor purchased land to the northeast of the agricultural property to move the business he operated, National Twist Drill & Tool Co., from Detroit to Oakland County. (Courtesy of the Williams family.)

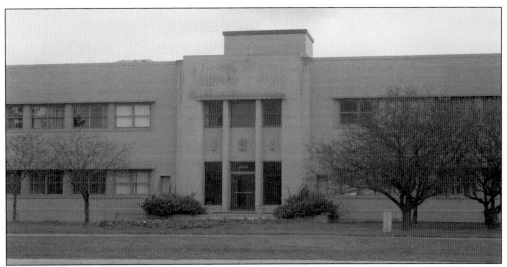

The National Twist Drill & Tool Co. moved north in the 1940s and developed into a 650,000-square-foot facility. At first, some residents were leery of heavy industry coming to Rochester but soon well-paid skilled labor jobs convinced residents that these industries were valuable to the community. During World War II, the company created the machines that manufactured armor plate for battleships. By some accounts, they provided 95 percent of the Navy's metal-cutting tools during this time. (Photographed by the authors.)

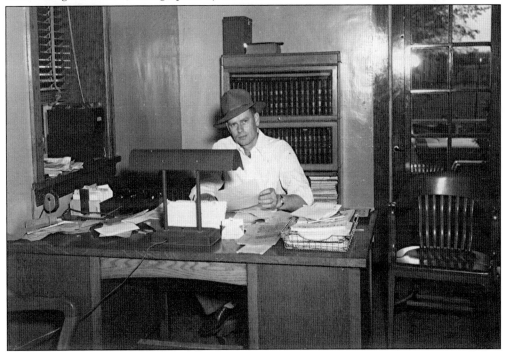

Robert Williams was an Angus expert who moved with his family from upstate New York to manage the farm and breeding program for Howard McGregor Sr. Seen here in the farm office, "Bob" always insisted that the office be kept clean and tidy, asking his secretary to keep the woodwork nicely polished. The office was to reflect the reputation Great Oaks Stock Farm enjoyed nationally. (Courtesy of the Williams family.)

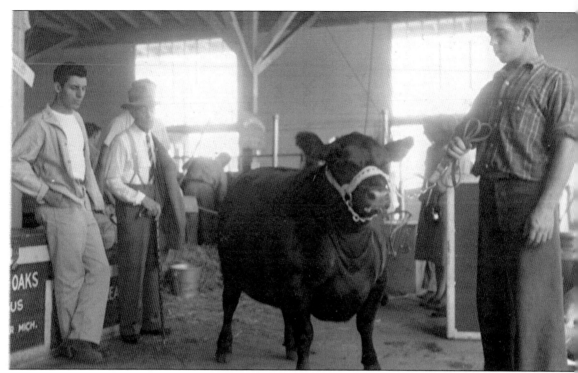

In 1947, Lucy the heifer was an early standout at the Michigan State Fair. Angus cattle are judged by many standards, one of which is the angle of their back, which is supposed to be straight. It was an angle that was often manipulated in photography for professional journals. To accomplish this feat, a shallow pit was dug in which to place the cattle's hind legs, lowering her rear by a few inches and increasing the appearance of a straight spine. The photograph was taken and retouched to make it look as though there was hay around the animal's feet, which instead hid the fact her feet were below ground. Practices such as this were commonplace, even in the days before software like Adobe Photoshop. Though Lucy was a winning heifer, she was not perfect enough for a photographic journal. (Courtesy of the Williams family.)

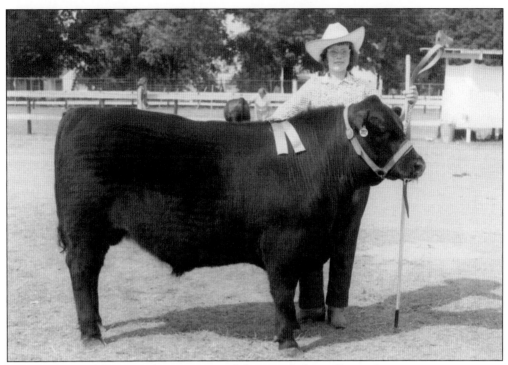

Great Oaks Stock Farm cattle were so prized that people from all over the country came to view and purchase them at an annual auction held at the farm. In the 1950s, a senator from Tennessee came to view and bid on some of the livestock offered. The senator's name was Albert Gore Sr., the father of Al Gore, vice president of the United States. Robert Williams's daughter Roberta Jane is seen here with a prized steer that she raised and showed herself through participation in the 4-H Club. (Courtesy of the Williams family.)

Howard McGregor Sr. purchased portions of the Ferry-Morse Seed Company after it moved away from Rochester in 1959, expanding the family's land holdings to around 1,800 acres. He employed many local farm hands, some seen here standing with Robert "Bob" Williams, who ran the farm operations. Upon the death of McGregor, ownership of the Great Oaks Stock Farm herd was passed to Williams. (Courtesy of the Williams family.)

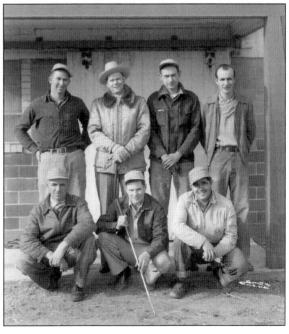

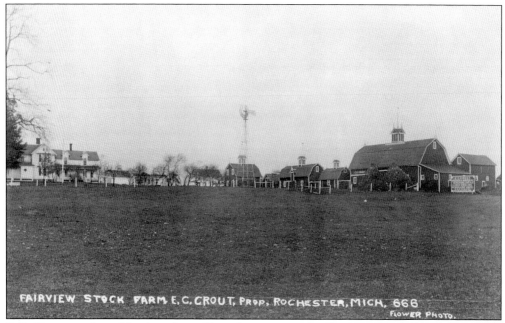

E.C. Crout purchased land in Avon Township to start the Fairview Stock Farm. Originally purchasing 65 acres, he continued to purchase land and grow the property until 1914, when he started to sell off plots. He sold approximately 103 acres to Frank Parmenter in that year, then Parmenter sold the parcels to A. Moore in 1916.

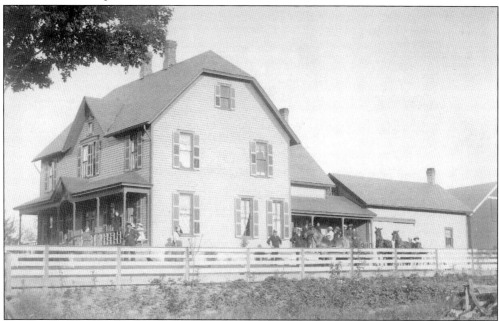

The son of German immigrants, John Tienken was a Holstein dairy farmer who was born here in 1864. In 1909, he and his friends established a local dairymen's cooperative called Rochester Creamery, of which he was the director. Civically, he also was active on the board of Ross School. After his death in 1944, his property was carved into more than 13 subdivisions with some 263 lots, a testament to the size of his agricultural holdings. (Courtesy of Rochester Hills Museum.)

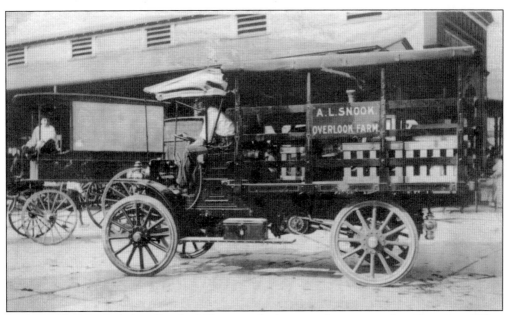

Rochester farmers including Overlook Farm supplied surrounding areas such as Detroit and Flint with produce. The John J. Snook family owned Overlook. Their Clark truck is shown delivering goods at Eastern Market by shed No. 2, like it would have throughout the harvest season. There were three markets in Detroit: Eastern Market, which opened in 1891 and is still in existence; Western Market, which closed in 1965; and Chene-Ferry Market, which closed in 1990. (Courtesy of Art Snook.)

A NEW YEAR

Time says a New Year now is here;
    May actions true with kindness blend,
Shining from each glad page of cheer
    To brighten days for you, dear friend.

                              JOHN J. SNOOK.
Rochester, Mich., Jan. 1st, 1923.

John J. Snook had many talents and was an accomplished poet. Often thought of as the unofficial poet laureate of Rochester, his charming collections of poetry were published and available locally for purchase. This image of a jaunty and cheerful card he created for the New Year shows the depth of his poetic charms. (Courtesy of Art Snook.)

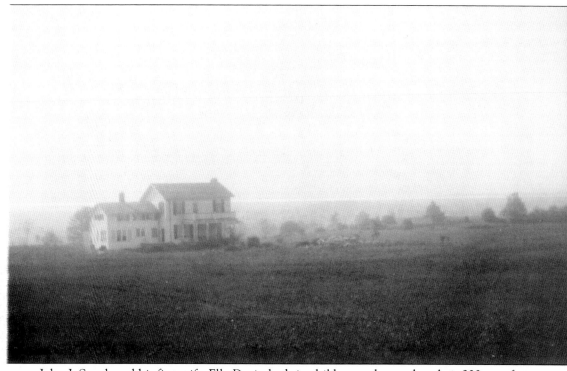

John J. Snook and his first wife, Ella Davis, had six children and moved to their 200-acre farm by Avon Road in Rochester in 1884. They named the farm Overlook for the idyllic views it offered overlooking the Clinton River Valley, just west of the city. Three of their boys became ministers and two went into farming, including Arthur L. Snook. Arthur was a prominent and much-admired Rochester resident who married Mary Newberry, a Rochester resident whose family owned farm property nearby. John's daughter, Nellie, purchased a farm near her family on Avon Road and made it her life's work to take care of the Snook family. John's son Arthur L. Snook also purchased a property nearby overlooking the same valley. They called their farm BerryNook Woods, combining the Snook family name with that of his wife's family, Newberry. They added the Woods because most of the property was wooded. The Clinton River Valley explodes with color every autumn, although the views afforded by both properties would have been beautiful year-round. (Courtesy of Art Snook.)

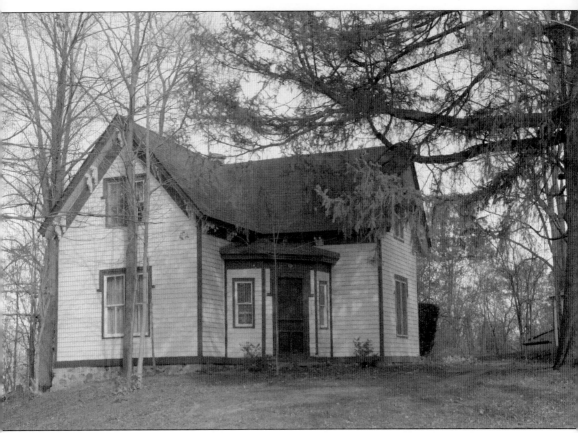

Arthur L. Snook married Mary Maxwell Newberry. Her father was Milo Prentis Newberry, a successful farmer and owner of a sawmill on the Clinton River that operated during the winter. He built this home just east of Rochester with lumber from his mill in 1863. Not only did he mill wood, he was also a talented cabinetmaker. Today, the Snook family is the proud owner of many of his original pieces, sure to be treasured throughout the centuries. (Photographed by the authors.)

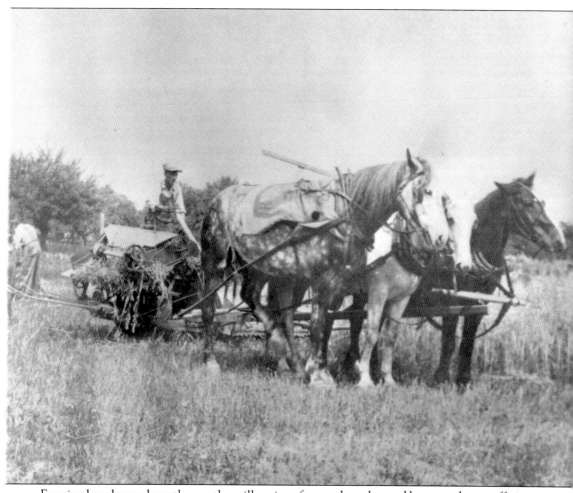
Farming has changed greatly over the millennia as farmers have learned better and more efficient techniques for increasing crop yield. Before mechanized farming, the laborer was heavily dependent on beasts of burden if he or she needed to farm large parcels of land. This image is of a horse rig cutting hay. (Courtesy of Rochester Hills Museum.)

Three
BUSINESS AND INDUSTRY

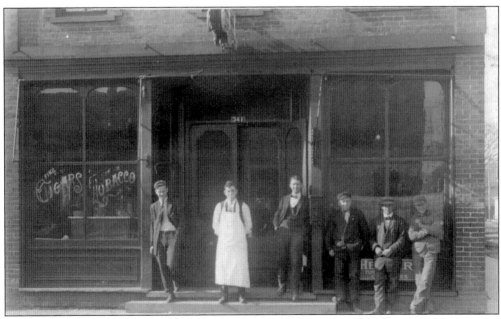

Many of the early businesses in Rochester were just as important for their social function as for what they sold. After the Civil War, the local Grand Army of the Republic chapter, which consisted of veterans of the Civil War, met at this location. Understandably, it was a tobacco shop—a good place for men to meet and discuss politics, business, and memories.

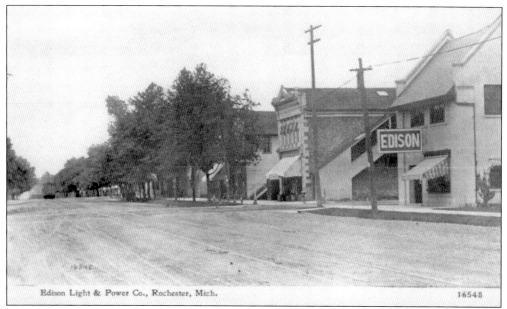

In 1897, Ambrose Bettis installed an electric generator using the Willcox millrace. Two years later, his contract to supply city power was revoked when the electric interurban arrived in town, its company offering a much better deal on electricity. This new electric company was soon incorporated into the Detroit Edison Company.

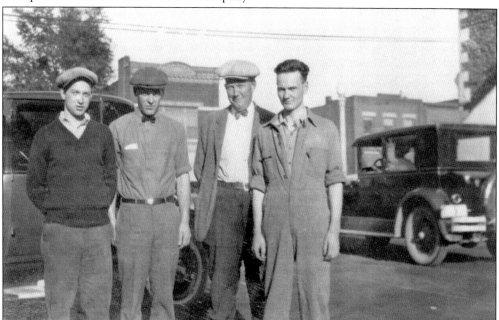

The Detroit Edison Company built its local headquarters on the southeast corner of Third Street in 1909, filling every letter of its sign with standard lightbulbs, which was quite an advertisement. Imagine how often residents saw employees standing on a ladder changing bulbs! This 1925 photograph shows members of the Detroit Edison Company's Rochester substation crew. Pictured are, from left to right, Ralph Crawford, unidentified, ? Corwall, and Tom Guest. Electrical service was popular, as the Michigan winter days were especially short. (Courtesy of Rochester Hills Museum.)

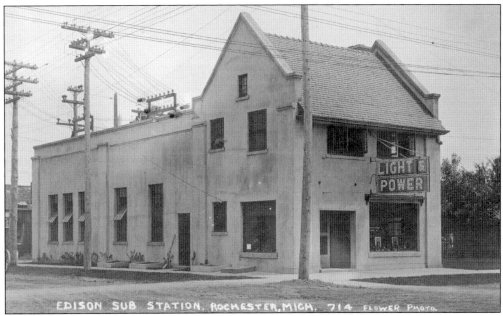

Electricity greatly enhanced the quality of life for many communities. Before electricity was common, the structures people lived and worked in were designed with survival, and not just aesthetics, in mind. Rooms were laid out to make the most of natural light, and furniture even tended to be somewhat mobile so family members could move it closer to a window. Electricity, and gas light before that, allowed architects' imaginations to flow freely, unencumbered by the constraints of natural light.

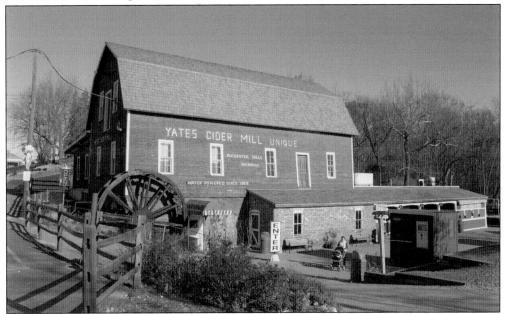

Nestled in the beautiful hills of Avon Township, Yates Cider Mill has been a tradition since 1876. The Yates family built a cider press in their existing water-powered mill that started its life as the Yates Grist Mill in 1863. Local farmers brought their apples to the mill for pressing after harvest. Today, the mill still operates much the same way it did more than 100 years ago.

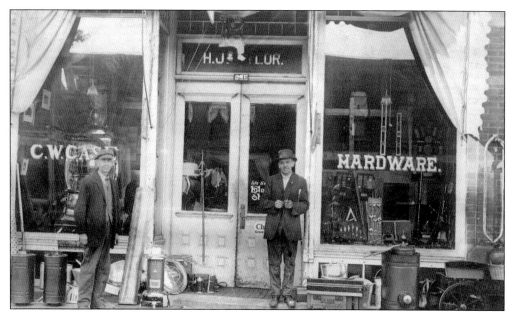

Built in 1885 by Joseph Reimer, this store (many times over a hardware store) changed owners throughout the 19th and 20th centuries. Charles W. Case worked at the store when it was owned by Harvey Taylor in 1897, but by 1907 Case owned it with business partner William Tienken.

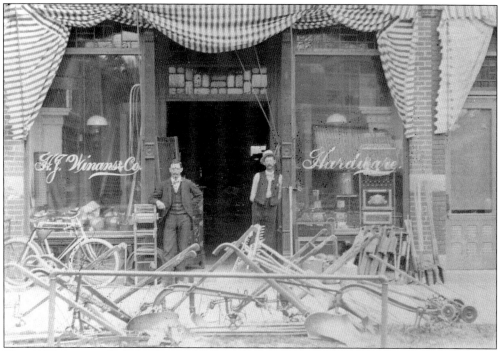

This 1905 photograph shows the same hardware store in the previous photograph with plows out front and Charles W. Case standing at the right. In 1915, Case and William Tienken separated. William built a plumbing store next door, and Case changed the hardware store's name to C.W. Case Hardware. The store burned in 1968. (Photographed by J.A. Boeberitz; courtesy of Rochester Hills Museum.)

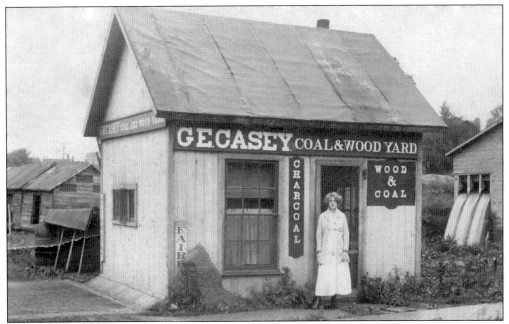

Elizabeth Butts is shown in front of her husband, G.E. Casey's, office building for his wood and coal company. The business concept seems outdated but at the time, wood and coal provided the only way to heat homes and cook food. Butts later divorced Casey and worked as a bookkeeper at C.W. Case Hardware, after which she married owner Charles W. Case. (Courtesy of Rochester Hills Museum.)

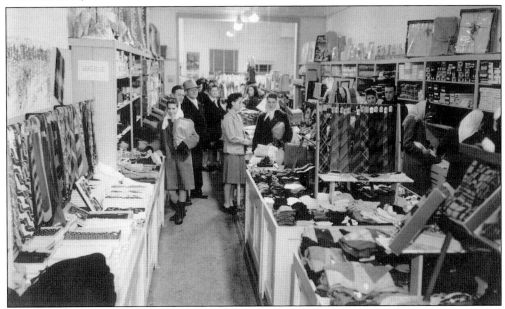

The building that housed Eggleston's Department Store also once held Murray's and Mitzelfeld's department stores. This photograph illustrates how much clothing stores have changed. Men's, women's, and children's clothing were in one store and not many options were available. For more unique pieces, women sewed their own clothes or took the DUR to visit Hudson's Department Store in Detroit. (Courtesy of Rochester Hills Museum.)

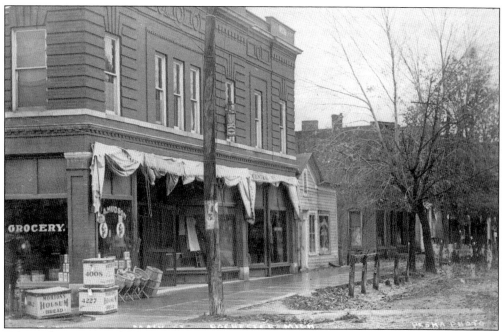

E.A. Hudson's was established around 1902 after Hudson decided to start a grocery in the town of his childhood, Rochester, carrying a range of regular and fancy groceries. This was not his only business. He was also quite successful in Detroit, where he owned Hudson Die and Tool Works. He lived on Oak Street.

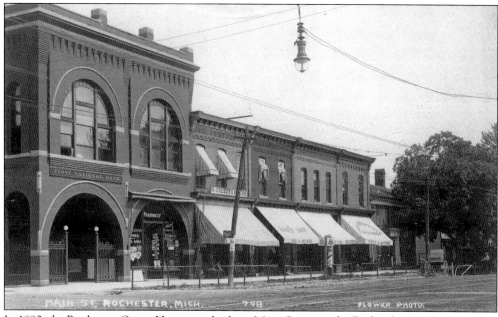

In 1890, the Rochester Opera House was built on Main Street in the Richardsonian Romanesque style. Although it never featured an opera, it did feature many local events on its second floor, like plays, graduations, and the annual firemen's ball. In 1917, the First National Bank and Norton Drugs occupied it. In 1925, the theatrical level closed because its floors were weak. Today, it is Lytle Pharmacy, a long-standing institution in Rochester.

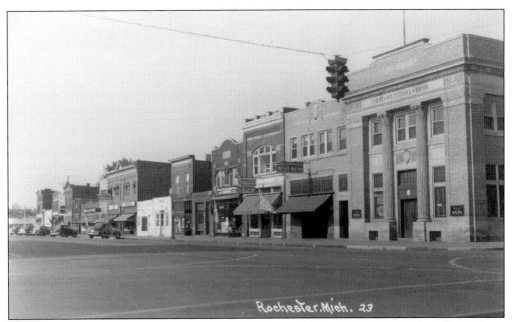

First National Bank was started by Charles Chapman, Charles Upton, J.C. Day, John Norton, D.M. Ferry, and Mr. McCotter. Many towns built hometown banks with local money to loan to local customers. First National Bank was created in this vein. It first occupied space in the Masonic block before moving across the street to this building.

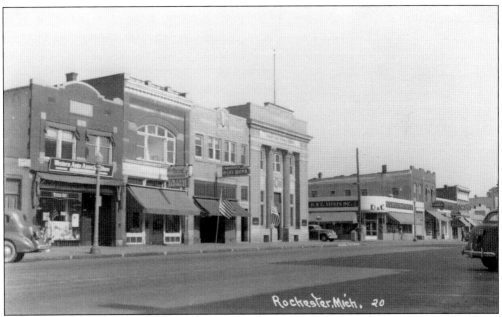

In the book *A Lively Town*, a story is related of a clerk named Milton Hazelwerdt. Charles Chapman hired him at First National Bank with the agreement that Hazelwerdt would get $75 a month, but if Chapman was satisfied with his work his salary would increase to $100 after six months. Considering Hazelwerdt retired as bank president sometime around 1960, he must have been successful!

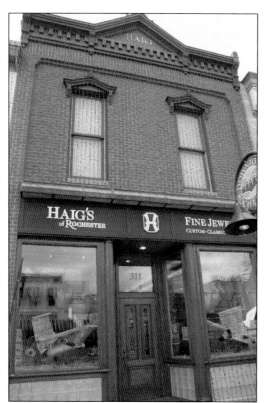

Who could have known that in the 20th century this structure, originally a furniture and undertaking business, would house Haig's of Rochester, a custom jewelry store that brings beauty to life? W. Harvey Greene built the masonry structure in 1882. He was the son of Calvin H. Greene, who once bought a photograph and book from author Henry David Thoreau. The rare daguerreotype of Thoreau he purchased is now part of the National Portrait Gallery's Collection. (Photographed by the authors.)

The old A&P is remembered fondly by many of the current residents of Rochester. The chain first opened in the Curtis building downtown in 1923, later moving north near Lipuma's Coney Island. This 1950s photograph shows large bags of Eight O'Clock Coffee and Bokar Coffee and also rows of cigarettes that were sold at two packs for 37¢ or $1.29 for a carton. To the right is a meat counter and cash register. (Courtesy of Rochester Hills Museum.)

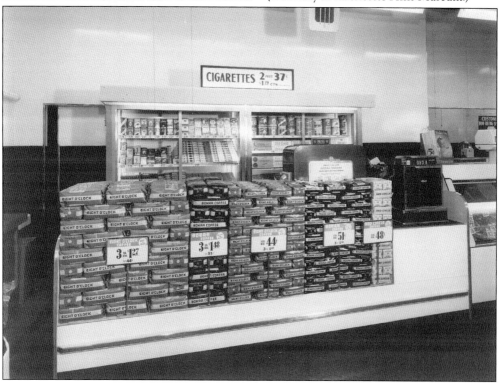

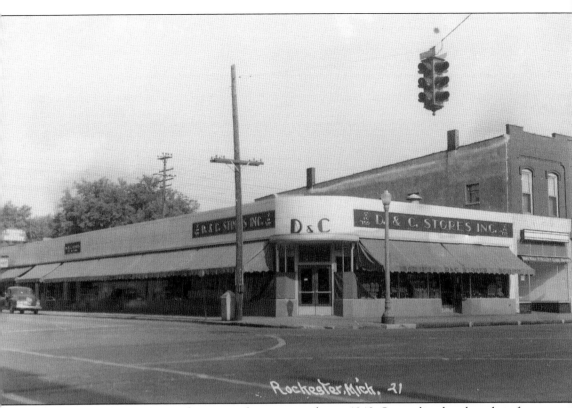

Above is the D & C Stores, five years after opening day in 1940. Streamlined and modern for the times, the store offered expanded goods, and the interior was a marked improvement over the previous space, which had been considered too dark and old-fashioned. This rehabilitation took place on the old Lambertson block. In 1945, the D & C Store shared the building with other retailers who used a separate entrance at the rear of the building. Over time, the discount store grew to encompass the complete building. Its expansive candy department fueled the dreams of a generation of Rochester children; it was a modern phenomenon as the concepts of childhood changed. Since then, many restaurants have occupied the space.

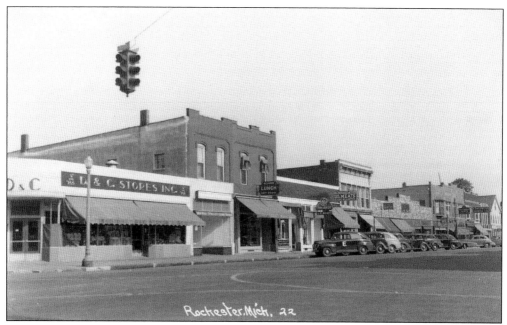

In 1926, the Dancer brothers and partner Glen Cowan founded the D & C Stores Inc. chain. The company started in Stockbridge, Michigan, but quickly expanded. The company existed for 67 years until competition from discount retailers such as Walmart drove it out of business. All 54 Michigan stores closed by 1993.

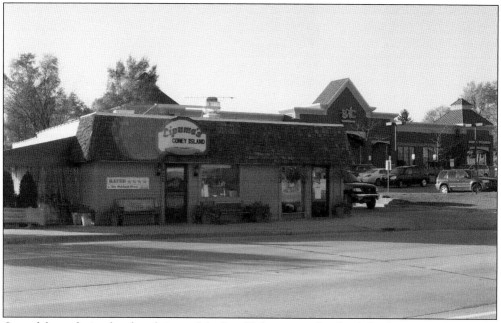

One of the enduring local traditions of the late 20th century that lends Rochester a unique sense of place is Lipuma's Coney Island, located on Main Street by the Paint Creek Trail. Coney dogs are a local Detroit rite of passage and Lipuma's has been proudly serving them for decades, often to long lines of customers. This is roughly the spot where the town's first mill stood in 1819. (Photographed by the authors.)

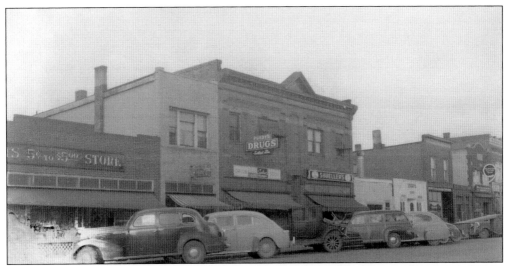

Purdy's Drugs was in operation for the middle decades of the 20th century. The owners, Henry and Elizabeth Purdy, owned a drugstore in Clawson before moving to Rochester where they purchased W.E. Ford's pharmacy at 321 South Main Street. Tom Hunter purchased it from them in 1963. Janet Varner Clothing for Women is in that building today.

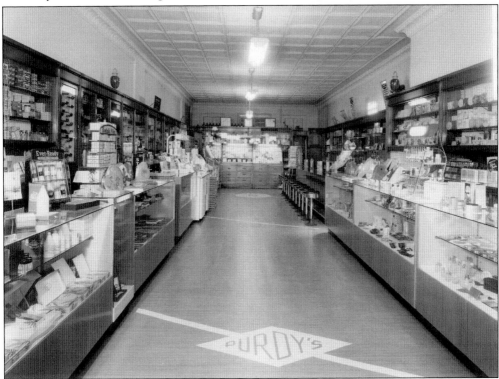

In the 1920s, soda fountains exploded across the nation, providing a new social outlet in the wake of Prohibition. In 1914, the Harrison Act prohibited the use of cocaine and opiates in these drinks, and they became the teetotaler-friendly "soft drinks" made of ice cream and syrups. Through the 1950s, soda fountains like the one at Purdy's Drugs were a popular youth hangout. (Courtesy of Rochester Hills Museum.)

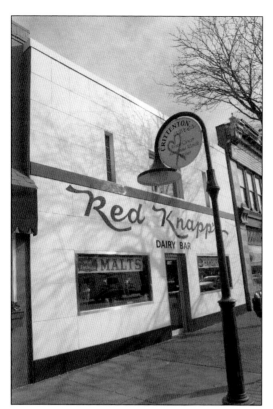

During the Great Depression, Red Knapp ran a gas station 24 hours a day, by himself. If customers needed gas at night they would ring a bell for his service. By the 1930s, Knapp had entered the restaurant business, serving classic American food. The iconic Red Knapp's Dairy Bar that is known today was built on top of a used car lot in 1950. It has a classic, mid-century style with a Vitrolite panel facade. (Photographed by the authors.)

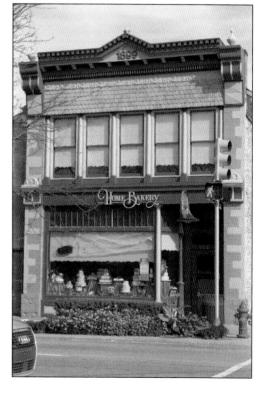

This building is the oldest commercial structure in Rochester, built in 1849. The cobblestone building on the corner of Main and Third Streets has a rehabilitated front facade that reflects its 1899 appearance. Dr. Rollin Sprague, the builder and first owner, originally opened a drugstore in this building. (Photographed by the authors.)

The Rochester Elevator is one of the city's preservation success stories. Built in 1880, it was repainted in 2009 and today is a cherished part of downtown. Originally it was one of two grain elevators built by C.K. Griggs and his brother A. Griggs. Grain elevators use gravity to scoop, elevate, and deposit grain into storage. (Photographed by the authors.)

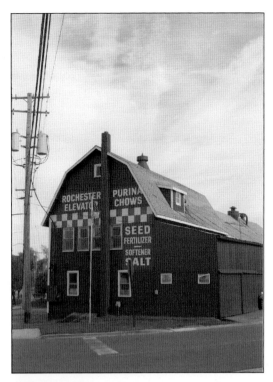

In 1938, when labor disputes within the grocery chain Kroger were at their height, union organizers brought their crusade to Rochester. These eight men were picketing the downtown store when a fire alarm went off in another area of town, drawing away police. While the policemen were occupied, local townspeople ran the picketers to the river and threw them in. Not to be outdone, the next day organizers showed up with 50 picketers. Labor laws in all fields continued to solidify throughout the 20th century.

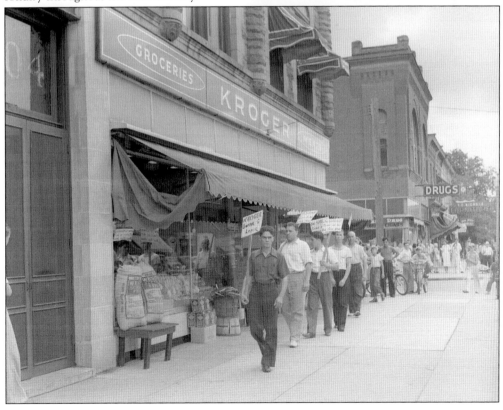

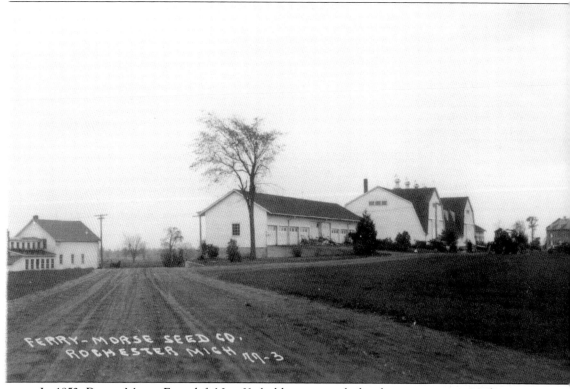

In 1852, Dexter Mason Ferry left New York, like so many before him, to move to Michigan in search of higher wages. He took a job as a bookkeeper at the American Seed Store and within a few short years became a partner. By the time the group had outgrown its home in Detroit in 1902, the D.M. Ferry Company, as it was then called, found land in Avon Township on which to expand its operations. Focusing on supplying regional prepackaged seeds for home gardens, the company eventually moved completely to this agricultural region. It swelled to 850 acres and shipped fresh seeds around the world. Ease of transportation and the creation of packaged seeds tailored to local growing conditions made this seed company an early success.

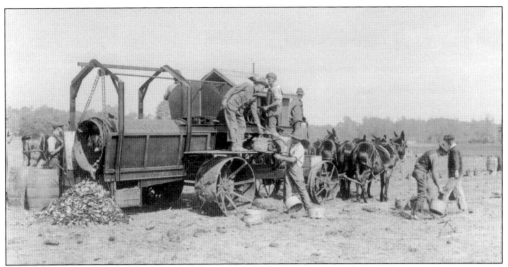

By 1929, the D.M. Ferry Company merged with the C.C. Morse Company of California to become the Ferry-Morse Seed Company of Detroit and San Francisco. Blending the two companies made perfect sense as the Morse Company, previously owned by R.W. Wilson, had been busy since the 1870s producing high quality seeds for D.M. Ferry and his original partners. Workers are shown here cultivating fields.

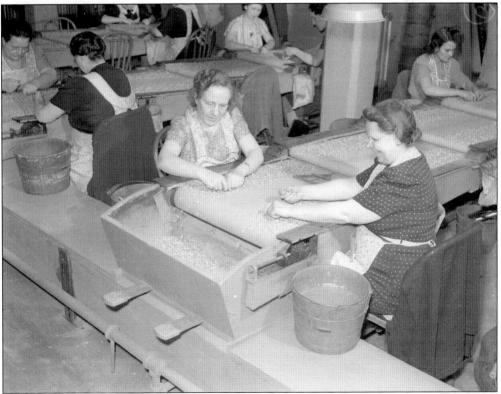

With industrialization came division of labor, especially between genders. Women are seen in the Ferry-Morse Seed Company sorting seeds, a job many thought women were better at because of their smaller hands. (Courtesy of Walter P. Reuther Library.)

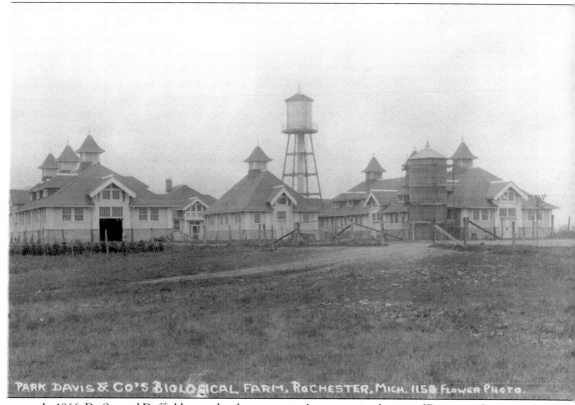

In 1866, Dr. Samuel Duffield started a pharmaceutical company in the city of Detroit and partnered with Harvey Parke. At the time, Detroit was one of the leaders in the world in this industry. By 1867, Duffield and Parke took on a third partner, George S. Davis, but just two years later Duffield left the company. Parke, Davis & Co. was incorporated in 1875. Its lab was at the corner of Henry and Cass Streets in Detroit until it expanded in 1873 to the Parke-Davis campus on the Detroit River. Today, one building, the 1902 laboratory, has been rehabilitated as the Omni Hotel. Once the largest company of its type in the world, Parke, Davis & Co. was a pioneering force in the development of pharmacologic and physiologic standards for pharmaceuticals. This image shows the barns on its rural Avon Township property that it purchased in the early 20th century.

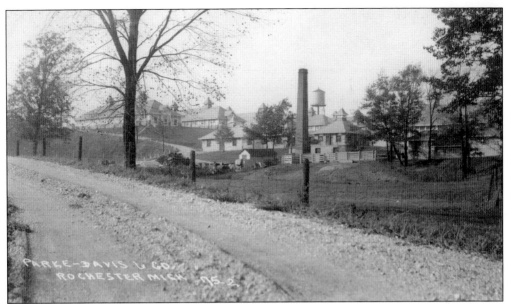

As the business grew, Parke, Davis & Co. needed to house its ever-increasing inventory of testing animals that were needed to research and develop vaccines. Detroit was too urban, so the company purchased 340 acres in 1907 in Avon Township and named the new farm Parkedale. By 1909, the farm had 150 sheep for serum, 200 horses for antitoxin for diphtheria and tetanus, and many cattle, which were used in smallpox research. The road leading up to the barns shows how idyllic the location truly was.

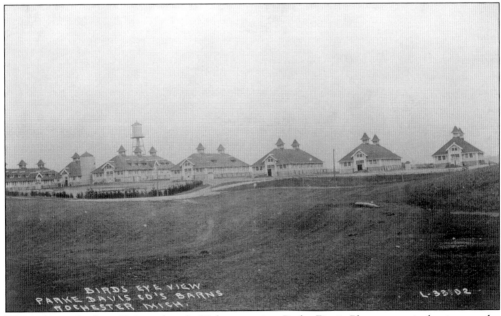

Throughout the late 19th and early 20th centuries, Parke-Davis Pharmaceuticals pioneered a number of products, including the first bacterial vaccine and the first widely available treatment for seizures. By the end of World War II, the company was instrumental in popularizing anti-infectives and developing the Salk polio vaccine. This is another view of the Parke-Davis barns.

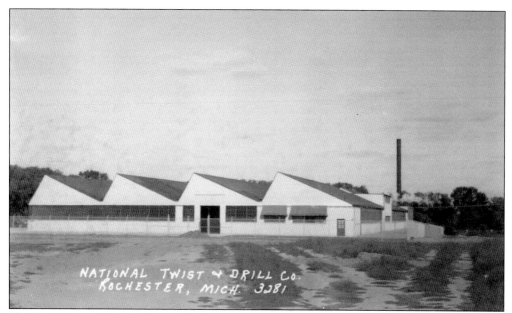

The National Twist Drill & Tool Co. symbolized the shift Rochester made in the 19th century from a rural agricultural community to a bedroom suburb of Detroit with its own burgeoning manufacturing industry. New commuters did not have to go into the big city to find well-paid manufacturing jobs anymore; they could be found right in their own backyard. This is one of the company's original buildings.

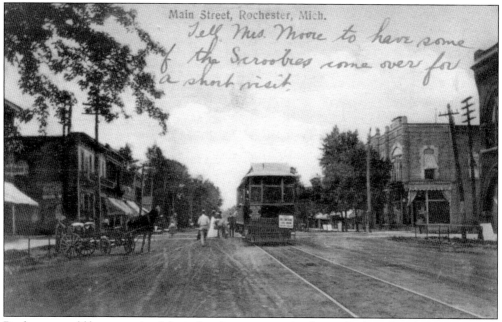

Rochester would have remained the isolated community that James Graham founded in 1817 if not for improvements like the Detroit United Railway (DUR). Invented in the 1890s, the interurban used overhead electric wires for power and ran on tracks like a train. Running down the center of the road, riders had immediate access to many regional locales, facilitating the idea of easy mobility. The car had a list of stops on the back.

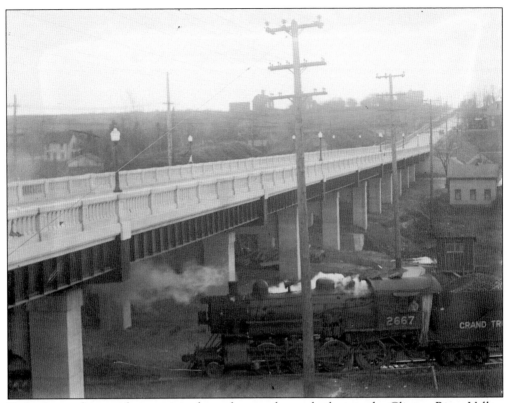

To lay interurban tracks an original wooden trestle was built over the Clinton River Valley. Because the grade was so steep, the train could not navigate the valley's span unless ground was built up on both sides. The concrete bridge that followed is seen here in 1927. The DUR track was originally built by the Detroit and Lake Orion Railway and only later became part of the DUR. (Courtesy of the Walter P. Reuther Library.)

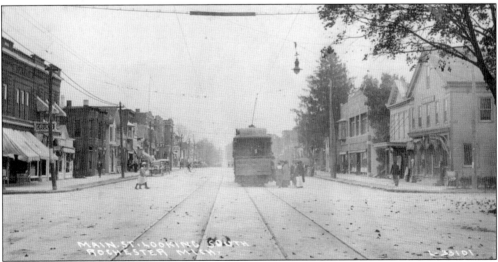

Here is another view of the interurban with riders getting on and off. Trams ran alongside the other key mode of transportation at the time, the horse and carriage. This image also hints to the future, with the tram sharing the road with an automobile.

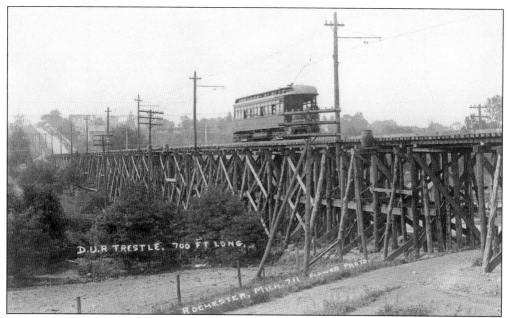

Considered "the people's train," the DUR traveled from Detroit right through the main streets of small towns, consolidating the Detroit area into a large community. Where the DUR entered Rochester at South Hill, a 700-foot trestle was built. Neva Crissman remembers the precarious-looking structure, saying, "Passengers always seemed quite relieved when they had crossed it going either way." This wooden trestle predated a concrete bridge.

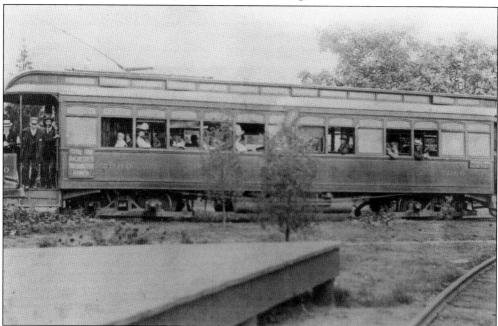

In this image of the interurban, a car filled with people is shown in great detail, revealing the personalities of the riders. Women wear the large hats of the Edwardian era, some engage the viewer, while others remain anonymous and continue about their business while the car is at a standstill. The men, especially the conductor, gaze back at the photographer.

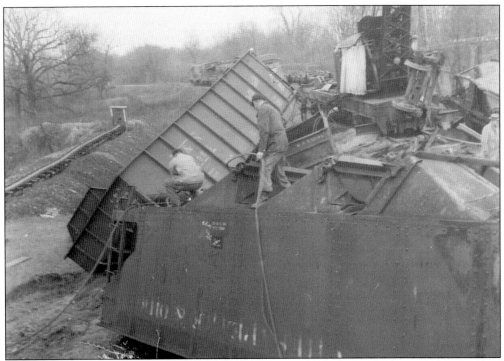

From their inception, trains were incredibly heavy, man-controlled machines, thereby holding the potential to be extremely dangerous. Though being restrained to tracks kept them relatively safe, mistakes are made even now. This photograph shows the workmen cleaning up one such early disaster in Rochester. In 1964, the Beeliner passenger train took its last trip out of downtown Rochester, making accidents like this less likely but also limiting public transportation. (Courtesy of Rochester Hills Museum.)

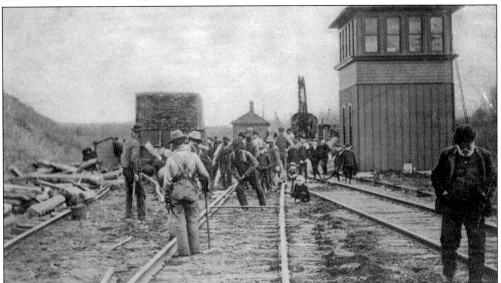

Even when a train was not at the junction of Michigan Central Railroad and Grand Trunk Railroad, it was quite busy keeping the vast infrastructure of trains viable. Maintenance meant many local jobs as tracks and stations needed regular repairs.

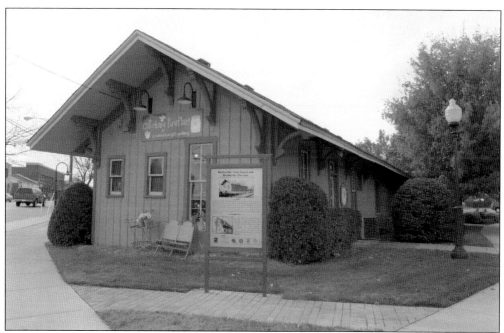

Built in 1880, this charming train station was used by the Michigan Central Railroad when the original line was purchased from Detroit and Bay City Railroad in 1881. Business was booming to such an extent in this small town that in 1907, approximately 30 trains a day came through the station. Although most freight stopped running by train to Rochester by 1960, passenger trains continued until 1964. (Photographed by the authors.)

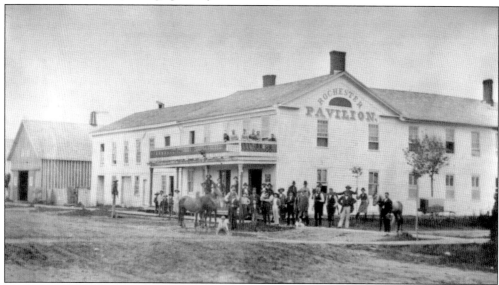

One hotel located in downtown Rochester was the Rochester Pavilion. It was a Greek Revival structure but with the gable end facing the side instead of the front, which was ironically the same style as its competition, the Lambertson House, which had a front gable. The Rochester Pavilion was on the southwest corner of Main and Third Streets and burned in 1887. It was replaced by the Detroit Hotel, which operated until it too burned in 1927, after which it was replaced by a Gulf Gas Station.

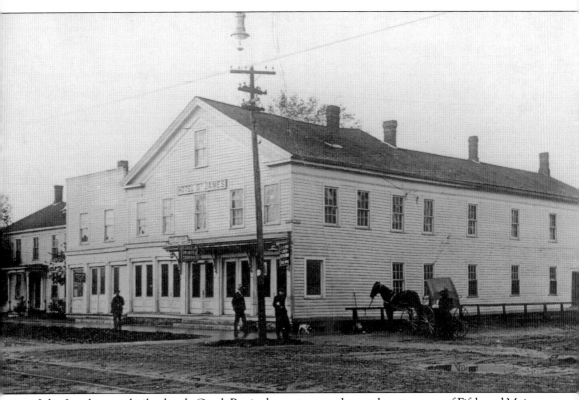

John Lambertson built a lovely Greek Revival structure on the southwest corner of Fifth and Main Streets in 1847, which he quickly sold. Many owners later, in 1861, a man by the name of Doc Lomason operated a hotel from the building that he called the Lambertson House. Hotels were especially important before the advent of trains and automobiles; slow travel prohibited people from moving quickly to their destinations. Stopping at a hotel allowed them to rest comfortably, buy supplies, and catch up on news. The building was also used as a hotel when Lomason sold it to another man, James W. Smith, who renamed it the Hotel St. James in 1890. The building continued as a hotel throughout most of the 20th century, but by 1962 it was considered dilapidated and was ordered to be torn down. By 1963 it was gone.

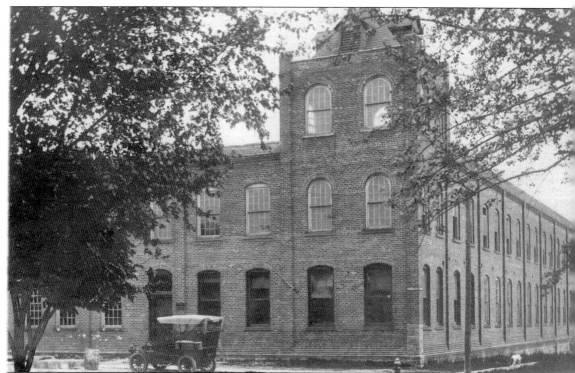

Transportation is incredibly important to industry. As modes of available transportation evolved, so did man's desire to be close to it. Ease of access in relationship to business helped make good businesses succeed. In the 18th century and before, proximity to waterways was essential, and with the development of train travel in the 19th century, locations near train tracks could be a matter of life or death for a company or town. Take the example of Stoney Creek and Rochester. Once the paths of the rail lines were decided, one town grew while the other remained static. Factories such as the Western Knitting Mill viewed location as essential, often choosing property on or near the tracks. Companies today tend to use current transportation patterns, such as highway systems, as a guide for their locations.

Four

Building a Better Tomorrow

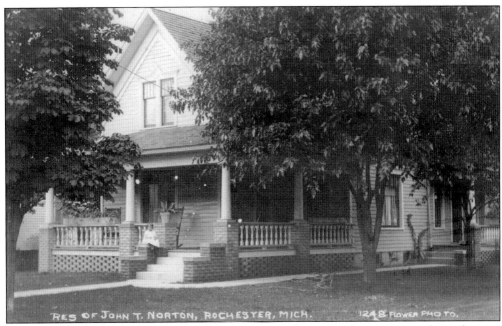

As railroads developed and crisscrossed the nation, people were no longer restricted to only using local materials to build their homes. Goods were moved quickly from manufacturer to customer and the development of building techniques in the late 19th century, like balloon framing, made the design and construction of many types of houses possible. This was the home of John Norton.

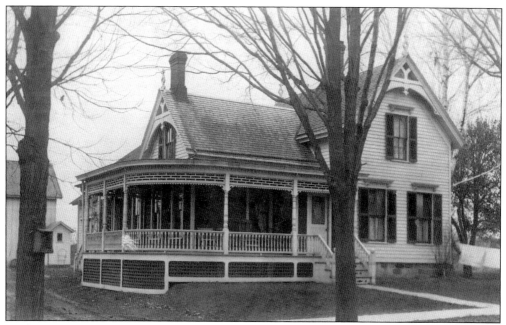

Rochester is fortunate to have many variant styles of domestic architecture from the 19th and 20th centuries. This home is a charming cross-gabled Victorian Queen Anne with a stunning wraparound porch. It is a spindle work subtype and has detailing on both the porch, seen in the slender balustrades and decorative frieze, and in the gables. Note the beautiful crest detail on the ridgeline as well.

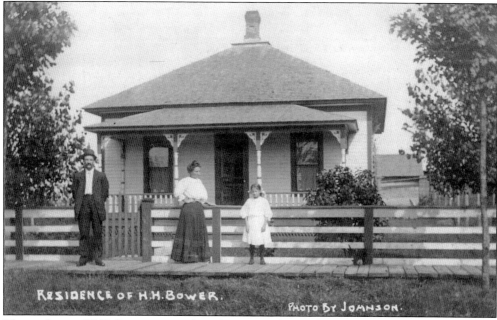

The residence of H.H. Bower is somewhat of a rarity in the northern states. Built in a Folk Victorian style, it has Queen Anne characteristics on a structure with a pyramidal roofline. Houses of this subtype are most commonly found in southern states like South Carolina, Texas, and Mississippi. They were mostly built between 1870 and 1910.

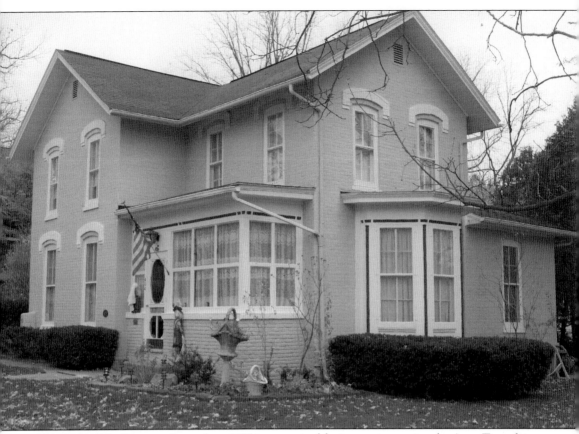

The George VanDeventer house from 1875 is recognized for its part in starting the Avon Township fire department. VanDeventer, three-time president of Rochester's village council, rebuilt this house after his previous one burned, all the while fighting for a public firemen's group. In 1882, he succeeded in gathering a volunteer group of men, but it was not until 1895 that the city formally recognized a firemen's group and granted funds for supplies. (Photographed by the authors.)

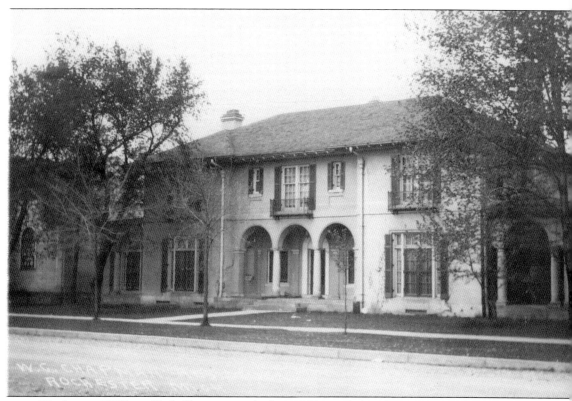

The home of William Clark Chapman was built in 1915 in an Italian Renaissance style, punctuated by the Roman arches of the front door. This house still stands today on Walnut Street just north of Third Street. Chapman, co-owner of the Western Knitting Mill, filled the home with fine furnishings and exquisite detail, showcasing his wealth and taste. Charles S. Chapman, William's brother and the other owner of the mill, had a large, stone, shingle-style house designed by famed Detroit architect Albert Kahn located north of Rochester on Main Street.

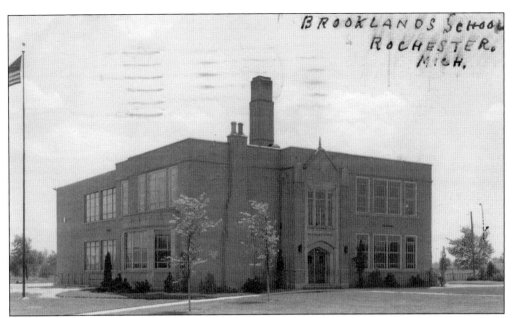

The Ordinance of 1785 outlined the divisions that new territories west of the Appalachians would follow, defined by areas called "townships" and "sections." A township was a six-mile square with further divisions of 36 identical sections in each one. Each section was 640 acres or roughly one mile. When these parcels were sold off, each township had one section retained by Congress to be used for public schools. From the very beginning of Rochester's settlement, a public education was hoped for. This image is of Brooklands School in 1941.

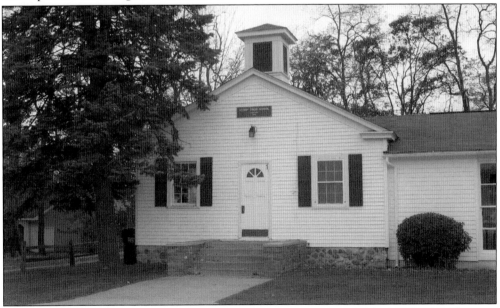

In 1825, the Stoney Creek community built a small schoolhouse for its children, with John Chapman teaching all grades. The 12-grade school, above, replaced the Stoney Creek school in 1848. It stands today as one of the last remaining public, one-room schoolhouses in the area. It is part of the Rochester Hills Museum at Van Hoosen Farm, and is used for interpreting Stoney Creek's heritage. Every third-grade student spends a day there to learn local history. (Photographed by the authors.)

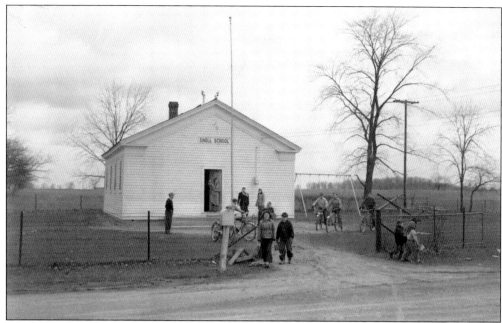

In 1951, Snell School had barely changed structurally but the quality and demands of the subjects taught to the students had transformed. Above, the teacher waves goodbye as children race off home. It is clear the school has been electrified, a major improvement from oil-lamp light. Below is the main room: to the left is a water cooler for the children with a basin behind that appears to have a drainage pipe but no running water. The former subjects of penmanship, spelling, and arithmetic have been improved upon and other subjects such as music, art, history, and others have been added as the years passed. Schools sought to provide children with a more expansive education in addition to preparing them for operating a farm or small business. (Courtesy of Walter P. Reuther Library.)

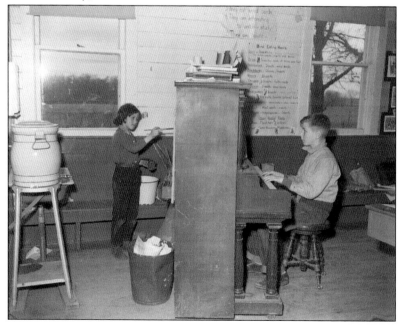

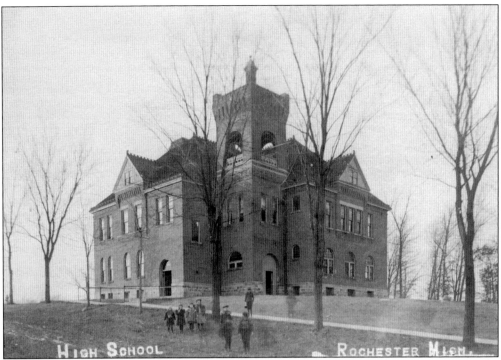

In 1823, Avon Township and village of Rochester children started their education in Alexander Graham's log cabin that was followed soon after by a schoolhouse built in 1828. One-room schoolhouses were a common feature dotting the 19th-century landscape and Rochester had many. As the population grew, so did the schools. In 1865, the community joined together to vote for an official board of education and a school tax. By 1888, the district had amassed enough funds to upgrade the run-down school on Walnut Street to the Harrison Building, a two-story brick building with indoor plumbing and a hot air furnace (above). Harrison is shown below in the 20th century with the first of many additions.

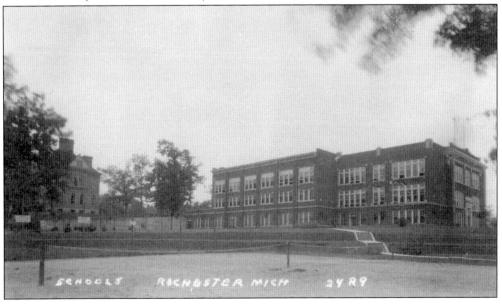

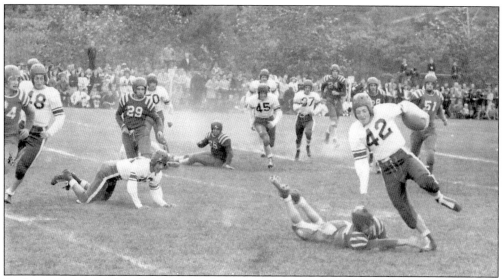

Rochester began to officially play football, baseball, and basketball against local schools in 1927. Since then, the boys and girls of Rochester have maintained their dedication and interest in sports. This undated photograph of the Rochester High School football team brings to mind several boys from Rochester who joined the NFL: Walt Kowalczyk in 1958, Charlie Sanders in 1968, L.J. Shelton in 1999, and Dominic Moran in 2007.

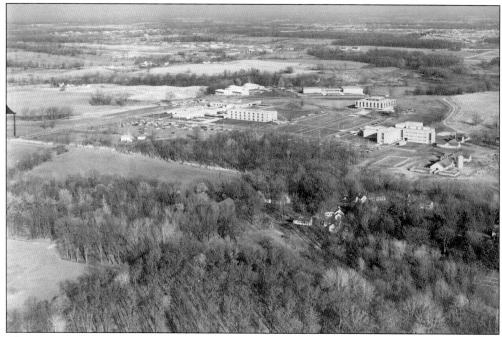

This 1957 aerial view shows Meadow Brook Farms in the foreground with the new Oakland University campus under construction in the background. In 1957, Alfred and Matilda Wilson donated their 1,500-acre estate, all their farm buildings, and $2 million to create an Oakland campus for Michigan State University. The first class of MSU-O enrolled in 1959. In 1963, the name changed to Oakland University, and in 1970 the Michigan legislature recognized the university by granting its independence. (Courtesy of Meadow Brook Hall.)

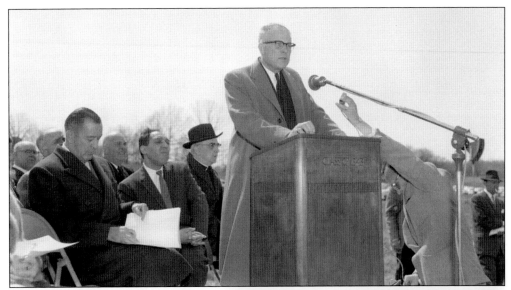

On May 2, 1958, the Wilsons and Michigan State University president John Hannah, above, broke ground for the new Oakland campus. The first buildings, Foundation Hall and Oakland Center, both dedicated in 1959, housed modest offices and classrooms. It was not until 1962 that the campus had a dedicated library or residence hall for its students. Oakland University represents one of the largest private gifts to found a public university. (Courtesy of Walter P. Reuther Library.)

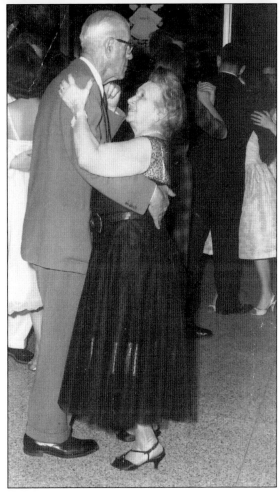

Like every project in their lives, Matilda and Alfred Wilson took a hands-on, enthusiastic approach to guiding the futures of students at Oakland University. Matilda often walked around campus, greeting students by name. She came to every graduation, every theater production, most campus events, and often held independent parties for students. This photograph shows Matilda and Alfred enjoying a slow number at the 1959 Christmas Dance. (Reprinted courtesy of Oakland University.)

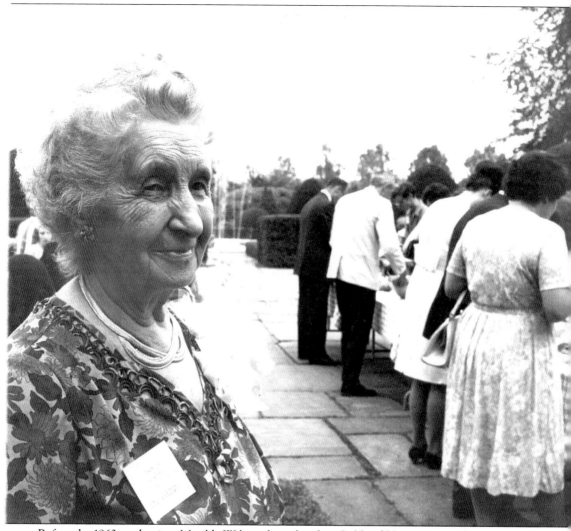

Before the 1963 graduation, Matilda Wilson threw her first Oakland University graduates a grand prom in the ballroom of Meadow Brook Hall. Having raised several children, Matilda understood that after a long night of dancing, a midnight breakfast would be well-received. The whole night must have been a magical experience; every effort was made so the students would have one last night to live freely and a wonderful place to say goodbye to the friends with whom they had reached adulthood. Matilda famously surprised each of the 125 graduates with a diamond graduation ring that night. She had a matching ring made for herself, which suggests the gifts were more than just a gesture. In 1964, she gave a reunion party for these first graduates. The pride she felt in their successes is evident in this photograph. (Reprinted courtesy of Oakland University.)

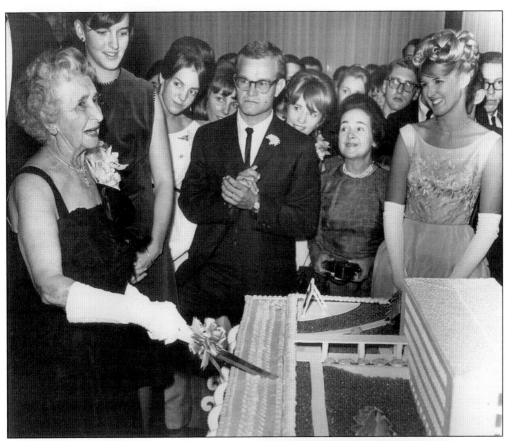

The first Oakland University students endured an unfinished campus but came to experience what had been named the "Harvard of the Midwest." Amazingly, they also became a surrogate family to Matilda Wilson. Under the guise of the Chancellor's Ball, the students at Oakland University surprised Matilda with an 80th birthday party in 1963. This tradition continued until her death in 1967. Her 82nd birthday especially represented her connection with the university, as the giant cake was topped with a copy of Wilson Hall, due to be finished in 1966. Matilda did not even know the building would be named after her, and being a humble woman, was extremely pleased to be so honored and respected. It is a mark of her and Alfred's characters that they did not name the university after themselves, which is an expected move when benefactors make large donations. (Reprinted courtesy of Oakland University.)

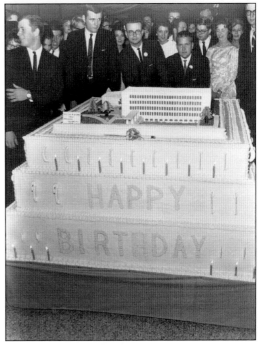

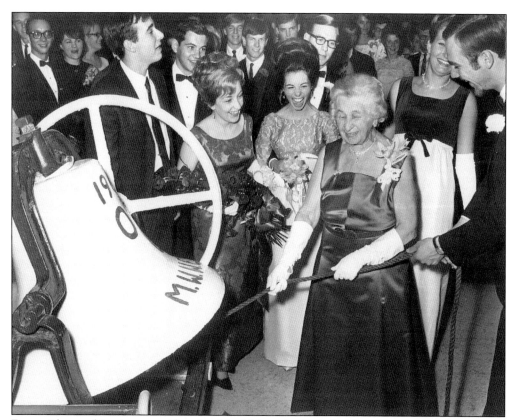

Even without taking into consideration Matilda's multiple philanthropic activities, she was well known for being a generous and altruistic woman, particularly towards the less fortunate. It is no wonder she was so well loved at Oakland University. This 1966 photograph shows Matilda celebrating her 83rd birthday, ringing a bell while she and the obviously enthusiastic students laugh at her efforts. (Reprinted courtesy of Oakland University.)

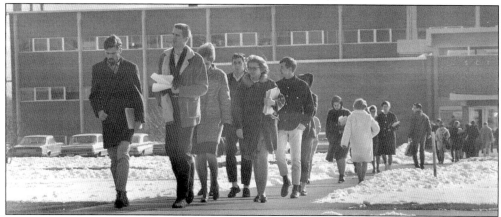

The first classes in 1958 were held in a former chicken coop, but slowly the campus evolved to its current 48 major buildings. Though a university, the campus is very easy to navigate on foot, as seen in this 1960s photograph of students in front of Hannah Hall of Science. Completed in 1960, it was first intended as a dormitory but is now connected to two science buildings, a combined 410,000-square-foot complex. (Reprinted courtesy of Oakland University.)

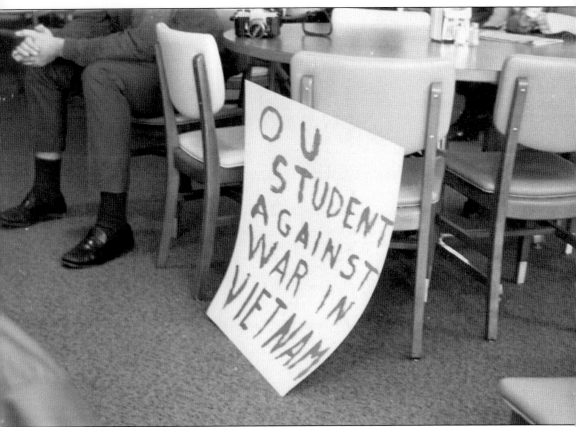

In 1959, Dean Robert Hoopes told the first students, "Our mission is to create well-rounded men, but men with sharp, abrasive edges; rebels with clear minds and uncowed consciences capable of being critics of society, not adjusters to it." Oakland University attracted many well-known and young professors who promoted free thought and a rigorous education. This poster from its 1967 GOP conference mirrors the nation's feelings about the Vietnam War and its consequences abroad and at home. (Reprinted courtesy of Oakland University.)

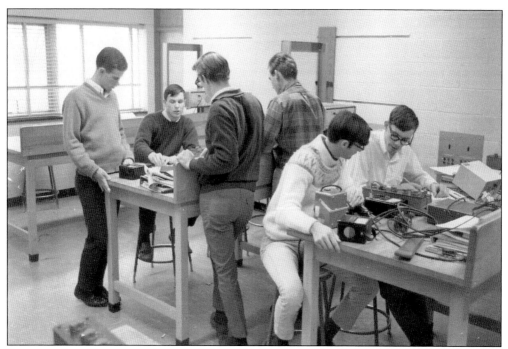

For more than 50 years, students at Oakland University have enjoyed a liberal arts education, as seen in this lab class. From left to right are Gordie Tebo, Jim Gray, Chuck Valerius, Mike Kalinowski, Jerry De Ruiter, and Dan Boayer. Students are encouraged to think, question, and experiment with the information they are given in class rather than to accept it blindly. (Reprinted courtesy of Oakland University.)

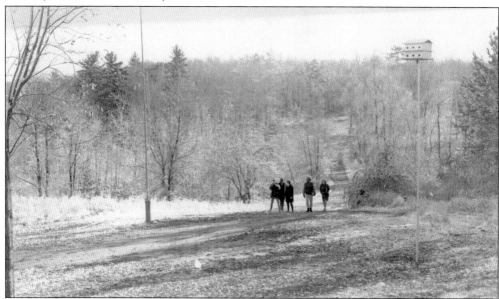

Oakland University remains a unique and unusual campus because of its natural beauty, which attracted dozens of farmers and later Matilda and John Dodge. The 1,500 acres were never completely cleared, leaving small stands of woods, meadows, and streams dotting the campus and making it a perfect place for an autumn walk. (Reprinted courtesy of Oakland University.)

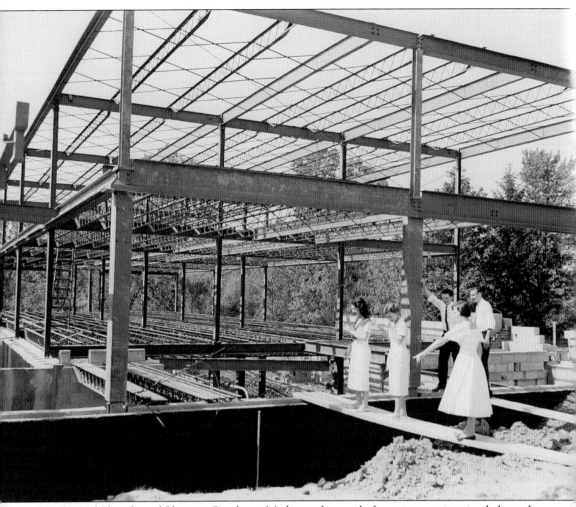

Members of Churches of Christ in Southeast Michigan dreamed of creating a university dedicated to Christian ideals in a liberal arts setting. In 1954, that dream became a reality when church members decided it was time to act and formed a board to investigate its creation. By 1957, funding had been secured and the Lou Maxon estate, down the street from the new campus of Michigan State University-Oakland, was chosen and purchased for the campus site. The Multi-Purpose Building, seen here, was built in 1959 and housed classrooms, offices, the cafeteria, and the dormitory. (Courtesy of Rochester College.)

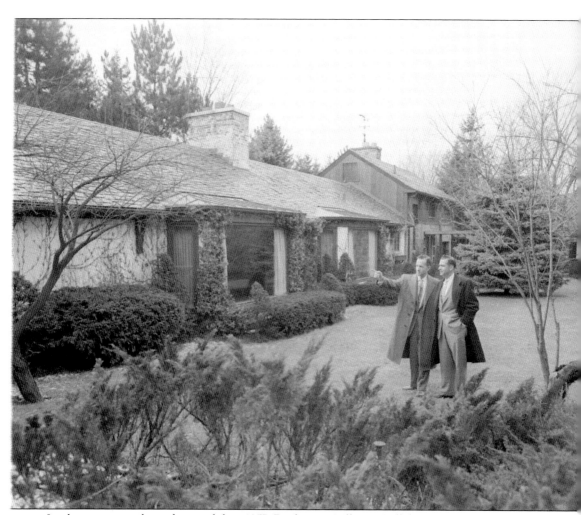

Looking very similar to how it did in 1957, Rochester College's Gallaher Center was originally the home of Lou Maxon. Maxon was a Detroit advertising agent whose home and surrounding lands were purchased as the site for North Central Christian College. This image of Wheeler Utley and Lester Allen on the property was first featured in the *Detroit News* in December 1957. The home, which first housed the college's library, chapel, and president's family, was named Gallaher Center in 1973. In the last 50 years, as the building's purpose shifted and transformed, much of its original woodwork was covered with paint and drywall. Alumnus Larry Stewart helped fostered an interest in preserving the building. He convinced the school that this "ugly" modern cinderblock building was not only important to North Central Christian College's (now Rochester College's) history but was also architecturally stunning. Many of the interior spaces have recently been restored. (Courtesy of Walter P. Reuther Library.)

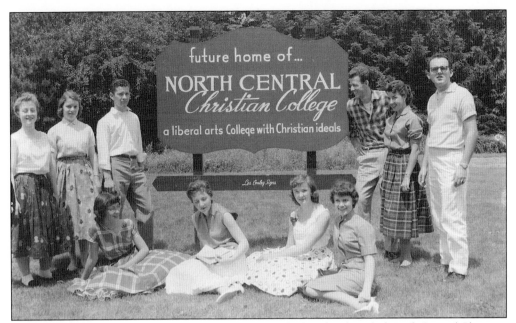

Starting in 1957, soon after the purchase of the property, the founding board of North Central Christian College began inviting local youth to open houses to entice them with the beauty of the property and the mission of the college. In 1958, they welcomed hundreds of teens, generating an interest in the new institution. Above are some of these visitors in a promotional shot. (Courtesy of Rochester College.)

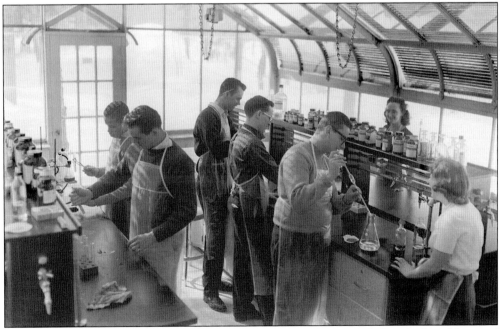

Early in 1960, the original greenhouse on the property was expanded with the addition of classrooms to become the college's first science building. The greenhouse structure, seen here, was used as the chemistry laboratory for one year. In 1961 and 1962, second and third additions were constructed to accommodate the growing student body and need for more class space. (Courtesy of Rochester College.)

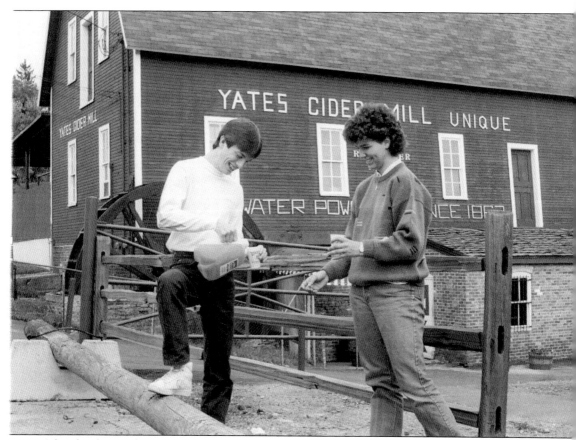

After developing the institution's first four-year degree program in 1978, North Central Christian College, now called Michigan Christian Junior College, underwent another name change, dropping "Junior" from the institutional name to become Michigan Christian College. The college graduated its first baccalaureate class in the spring of 1981. The Bible degree was the first of many four-year degrees the college added in the following years. As the area's population around the college grew and changed from a rural to suburban setting, the student body remained a vital part of the region. By 1997, the institution changed its name to Rochester College to better represent the institutional goals of "a liberal arts college in a Christian setting." Two students are seen here enjoying a favorite local fall tradition, apple cider at Yates Cider Mill. (Courtesy of Rochester College.)

The 1960s were a pivotal time for young Rochester College. In 1961, it started the new decade by changing its name to Michigan Christian Junior College, pursuing policies of diversification during the tumult of the civil rights era, and priding itself on winning its first men's basketball conference title in 1969. The college continues to outperform many larger schools in athletics, especially in men's basketball. (Courtesy of Rochester College.)

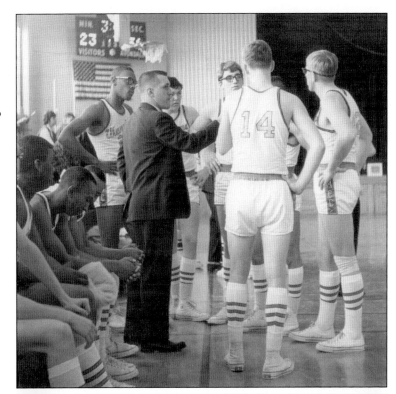

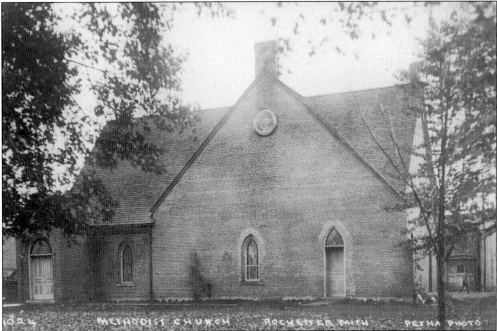

The first Methodist church was built in 1876 but had been organized some 10 years prior. The original meeting place was a schoolhouse the congregation purchased to worship in until it could build a more substantial structure. By 1913, it moved to a larger building on Walnut Street that is today the Masonic Temple.

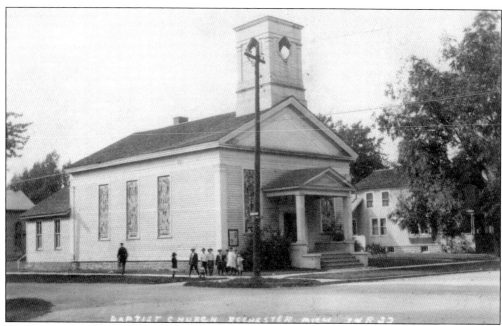

The Baptist church was the first church in Avon Township, started by Lemuel Taylor and Nathaniel Millerd in 1824. By 1855, the congregation had taken over an unfinished church in Rochester and completed it. In 1897, the church was very proud that it had added two new parlors to the building, and the changes did not stop there. As styles developed, so did the church. Based on the clothing, the photograph above was taken in roughly 1920 and the photograph below is from approximately 1945. These images show substantial changes since the church's first building. Images from 1897 and 1907 (not shown) indicate that in 1897, the church was a basic Greek Revival structure with a prominent steeple and louvered windows. By 1907, although the tower remained, the steeple was absent. By the 1920s photograph, the window treatment changed, the louvers were removed, and either stained or decorative glass was installed. In the 1945 image, the front facade was completely altered from the original: the steeple tower was completely removed, a large facade tower addition was constructed, and the original gabled entrance was gone.

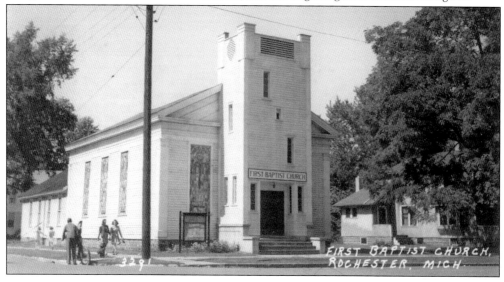

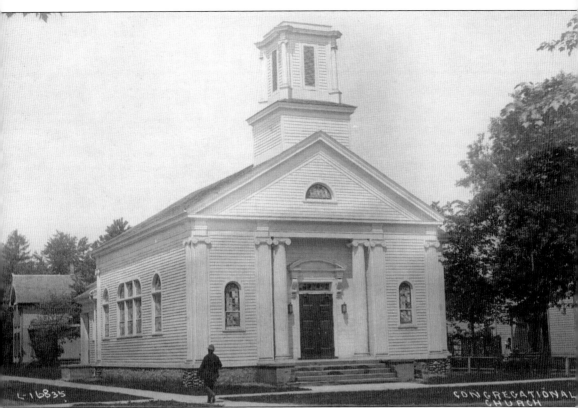

The Congregational church was built in 1854 at a cost of $2,600 and was dedicated on April 19 of that year. One of the oldest operating churches in Rochester at the time, it was established in 1827 and was holding services in a simple log structure as of 1839. It is still on Walnut Street, although today it is the home of a local business. This image shows the classic lines of the structure and the parsonage in the rear of the building.

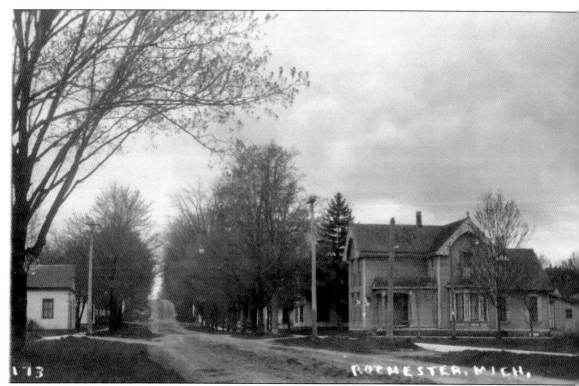

This Gothic Revival home comes from a long tradition of homes considered to be in a Romantic style. They are found particularly in the Northeast and the Midwest as families migrated westward. Part of the Picturesque movement, the style was a departure from the previously dominant classically inspired designs. Typically, they were built between 1840 and 1880. This home was built in 1878 as the parsonage for the First Congregational Church of Rochester and still stands at Pine and Third Streets.

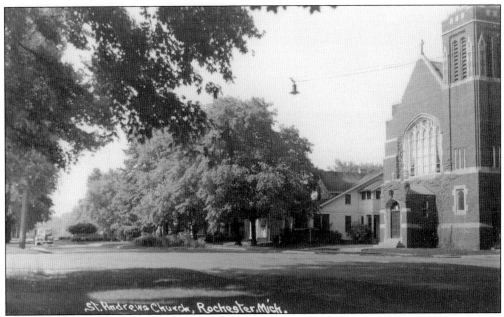

St. Andrew Catholic Church had an interesting beginning in Rochester because it was instigated by a non-Catholic. The Chapmans, owners of the Western Knitting Mill, convinced a priest to travel from Royal Oak to provide mass in Camille DeBaene's home for their Catholic factory workers. In 1928, this brick church replaced their temporary chapel. Through the 1960s, a modern church, convent, and eight-grade school developed north of town.

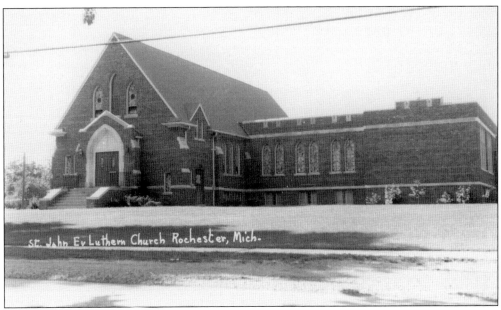

St. John's Evangelical Lutheran Church also had a shaky but impassioned background. In 1936, only 44 parishioners were congregants. In 1943, they began a school for area children, providing a faith-filled, strong education that continues today. Since the 1950s, the school has been located next to the church, pictured above, on West University.

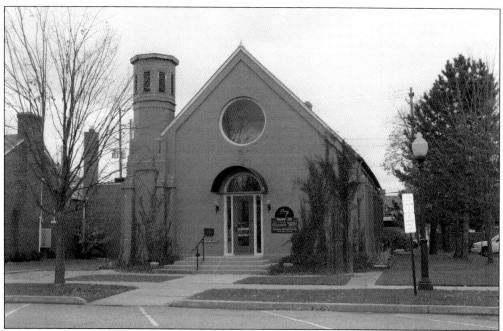

Organized in 1838, the Universalist church did not build this brick structure until 1881. The brick structure replaced the 1868 wood frame building that burned to the ground. Interestingly, in 1897, this church had a female pastor, S. Louise Haight. The Universalists were one of the first Christian denominations to ordain women as pastors. (Photographed by the authors.)

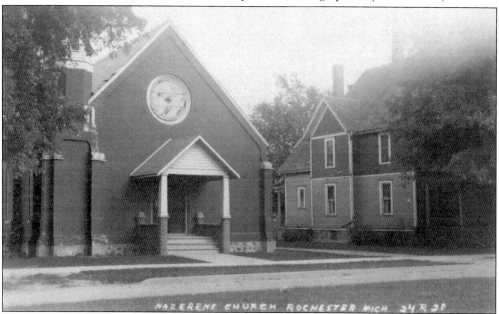

The Nazarenes moved into the old Universalist church on Walnut Street. The majority of churches in Rochester ran down this avenue, which is just one block west of Main Street. Many congregations have outgrown their original Victorian buildings, but they are still being utilized. The pews are replaced with gift shops and offices, a good reminder of the power of reusing and recycling historic buildings.

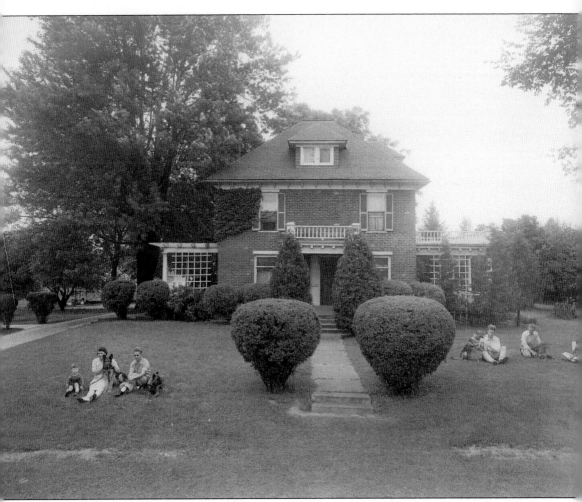

Guide dogs were successfully trained during World War I when the German government used canines for military applications. After the war, the German government decided to use them as service animals for returning soldiers who had lost their sight. An American woman named Dorothy Eustis along with Morris Frank brought this concept to the United States in 1929, creating the organization the Seeing Eye. This image shows an early class of clients with their leader dogs on the campus of Leader Dogs for the Blind, a non-profit that, like Seeing Eye, assists those who are visually impaired. (Courtesy of Leader Dogs for the Blind.)

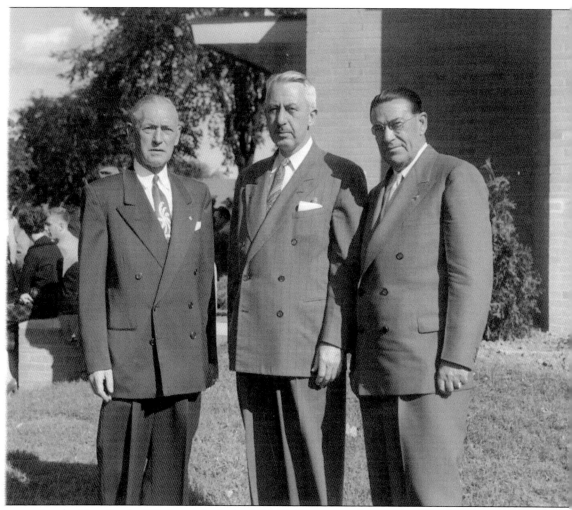

Leader Dogs for the Blind was the brainchild of a few extraordinary men. The founders are seen here, from left to right: Charles Nutting, Donald Schuur, and S.A. Dodge. The idea grew from a desire to help a friend and fellow Lions Club member, Glenn "Doc" Wheeler, navigate the world more effectively. Wheeler was rejected from the only other school in the United States when the Lions Club tried to pay for his entry into the program. (Courtesy of Leader Dogs for the Blind.)

In 1938, Charles Nutting, Donald Schuur, and S.A. Dodge went before the Lions Club members to seek support to help Doc Wheeler and they received it. They contacted Seeing Eye about procuring a dog, but to no avail. Having a feeling they could find a trainer on their own, they reached out to the community and found Doberman trainer Glenn Staines, who was willing to train four dogs to be used as guides. Pictured is Don Schuur with an early Doberman. (Courtesy of Leader Dogs for the Blind.)

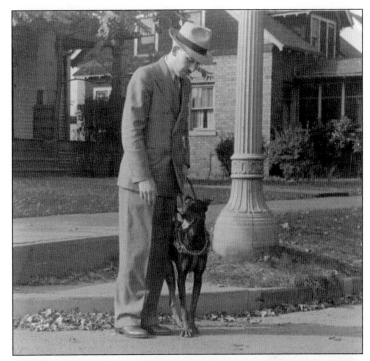

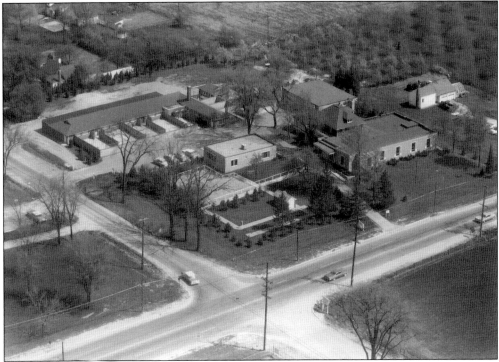

By 1939, Glenn Staines left Leader Dogs for the Blind (which was at the time called "Lion Leader") to start his own guide dog school. The remaining team searched for trainers and a property, finding one that year on a farm in Rochester. The aerial seen here shows the extent of the campus later in the century. (Courtesy of Leader Dogs for the Blind.)

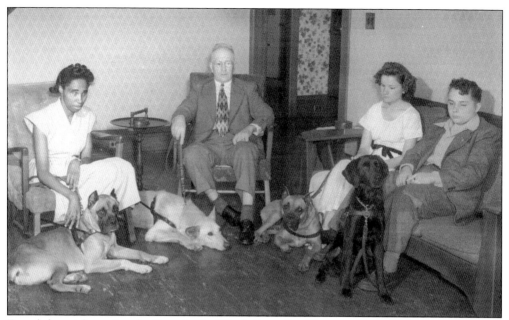

From left to right are Leader Dogs for the Blind clients Enid Bourne, Blair Smith, Geraldine Bios, and Richard Cullen during their 26-week training. The success of guide dogs across the nation has created a challenge when describing the animals. Many call all guide dogs "seeing eye dogs" when in reality, those are just the dogs trained by that organization. The correct term, no matter who trains the animal, is "guide dog." (Courtesy of Leader Dogs for the Blind.)

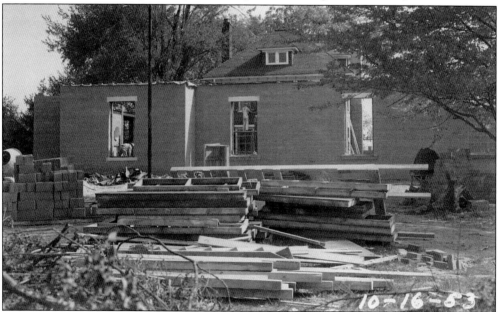

The original Leader Dogs for the Blind property utilized the masonry farmhouse, barn, and garages for the school. The director, instructors, and clients lived in the house, and the barn served as their first kennel for the dogs. As the organization grew, so did its need for space. This image shows construction of the first dormitories built on to the farmhouse. (Courtesy of Leader Dogs for the Blind.)

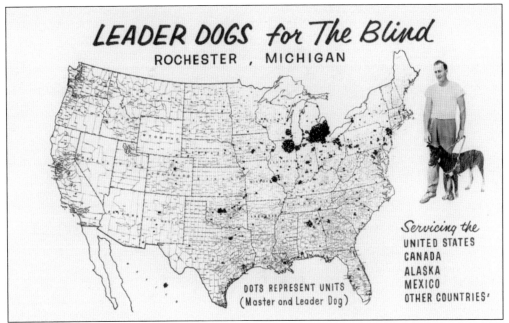

This map of Leader Dogs for the Blind clients, dating from around 1950, shows the extent to which the organization's reputation had grown. The Rochester property was probably successful for some part because of its central location in the United States. Although the qualifications for acceptance were challenging, clients from around the country and even the world came to Leader Dogs for the Blind for assistance. (Courtesy of Leader Dogs for the Blind.)

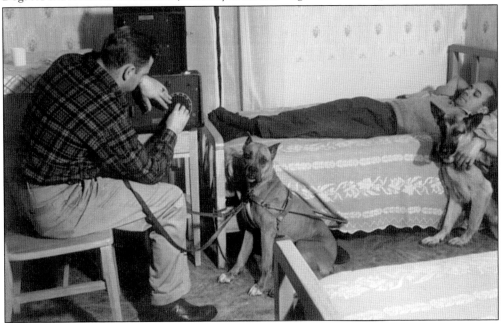

The accommodations for students then, as they are now, were top-notch. Two male students are seen relaxing in their dorm room. Each dog has to have its personality matched to that of a client so the staff can be sure the two will partner well together. More than 14,000 dogs have been placed with a human partner since 1939. (Courtesy of Leader Dogs for the Blind.)

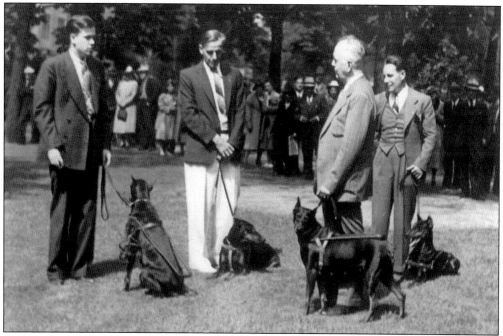

The first class for Leader Dogs for the Blind, seen here, graduated in the fall of 1938. Pictured are, from left to right, William Joyce, Earl Morrey, Dr. Glenn Wheeler, and Paul Brown. The first three clients were from Detroit, but Brown came from Toledo to get his training. (Courtesy of Leader Dogs for the Blind.)

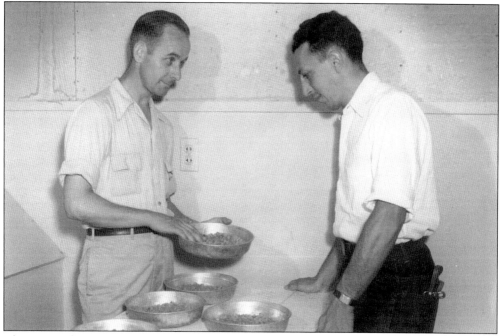

This image shows staff member Vincent Syracuse, who joined the team in 1948 and was the organization's field representative and dog trainer for more than 50 years. With him is Fred Maynard, the director of training. (Courtesy of Leader Dogs for the Blind.)

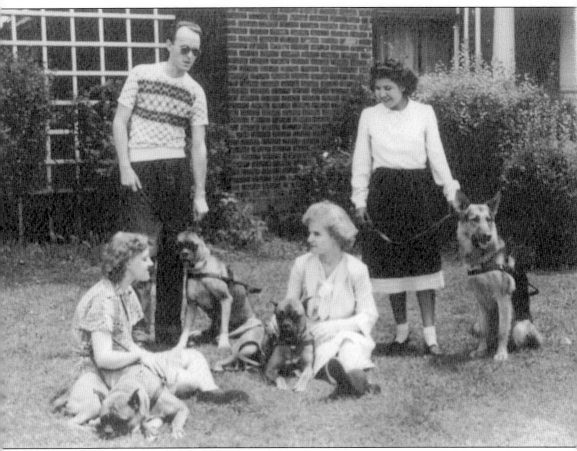

These Leader Dogs for the Blind clients are, from left to right, Ruth Carmen, John Teachout, Gloria Ristow, and Lilia Gonzales. The school has always been progressive. It was among the first to supply dogs to people who are deaf and blind, the first to provide services to the legally, not totally blind, and the first to provide dogs to Spanish-speaking clients. Other than the United States, Spain and Mexico have the most clients served. Dogs trained for the deaf and blind recognize and respond to hand signals and ASL with or without vocal support. (Courtesy of Leader Dogs for the Blind.)

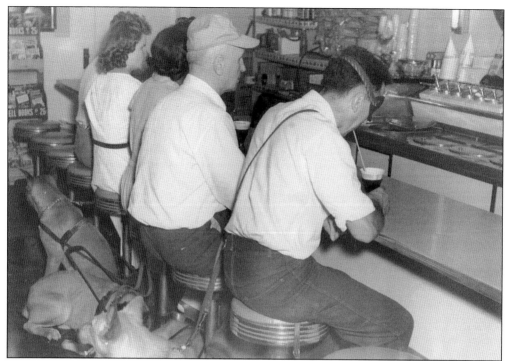

Red Knapp's Dairy Bar opened its doors early on so that clients and their dogs could train in a restaurant setting. Many Rochester businesses and residents have long been supporters of the Leader Dogs for the Blind mission. German shepherds, golden retrievers, and Labrador retrievers were eventually the preferred dogs for guide work as Dobermans were only single coated. That means training and work for Dobermans was much more challenging during the severe Michigan winters. (Courtesy of Leader Dogs for the Blind.)

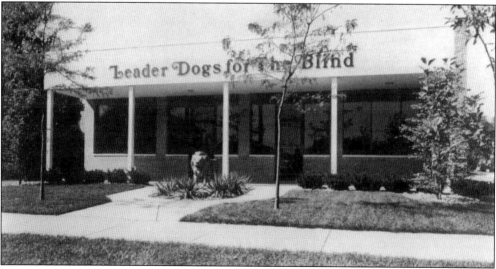

The organization continues to expand and reach more people who are in need. Currently, Leader Dogs provides US clients transportation to Rochester, a guide dog, and training free of charge through the support of sponsors and donors. This building in downtown Rochester extends training opportunities to both residential and city conditions. (Courtesy of Leader Dogs for the Blind.)

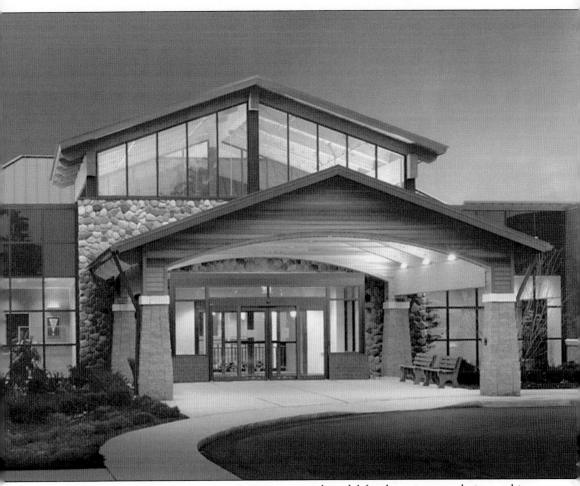

The Older Persons' Commission is a progressive social model for the aging population and is a vital part of the greater Rochester area community. It strives "to provide high quality programs and services that stimulate and advance active and healthy living for all ages of older persons." Senior Programs date back to 1956, when a group of men formed a men's card club that met at the American Legion Hall. In 1956, the Rochester Junior Women's Club asked the village council for a place where area seniors could meet and the council offered the Avon Park Pavilion. In 1983, the Older Persons' Commission purchased the old Woodward School building and most recently built its modern, state-of-the-art building at 650 Letica Dr. and opened in November of 2003. A variety of educational, athletic, cultural, and arts classes are offered. In 2009, the OPC was recognized as a Model Senior Center by the National Council on Aging. (Courtesy of the Older Persons' Commission.)

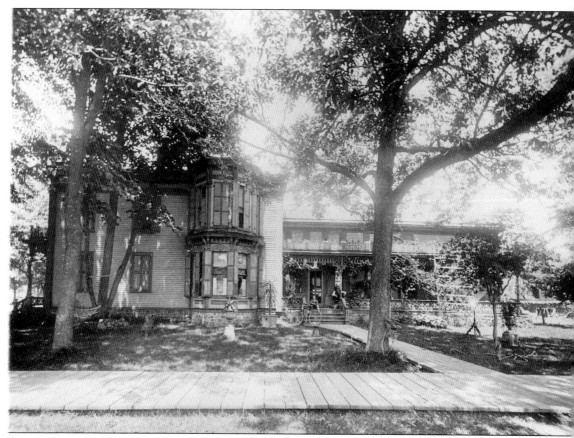

Almon Mack, whose father was a prominent colonel and entrepreneur in Pontiac, moved to Rochester in 1831. While in Pontiac, he ran a mill that supplied wood for the Bloomfield jail. He was part of the state legislature in 1848 and built this Victorian house at the corner of Third and Walnut Streets, which was demolished in 1934. The pale brick post office was built on the site, which now houses retail stores. Mack opened the second store in Rochester and was renowned as a kind and generous businessman by many citizens, not the least of which was Eliza Bromley. "Grandma" Eliza Bromley's memories of the War of 1812, life in the 19th century, and many of the main characters of early Rochester were recounted to the *Detroit News* and *Rochester Era* and are now in the Rochester-Avon Historical Society's archives. (Courtesy of Rochester Hills Museum.)

Five
MEN STURDY AS OAKS

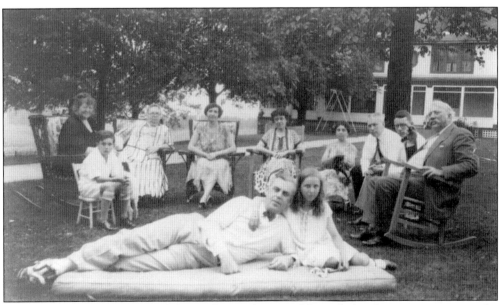

This image shows members of the Dodge, Wilson, and Rausch families on a picnic on the property of the Dodge farmhouse off Adams Road. Charming and idyllic, it was recreations such as these that convinced the Wilson family Avon Township was a good place to settle down and raise children.

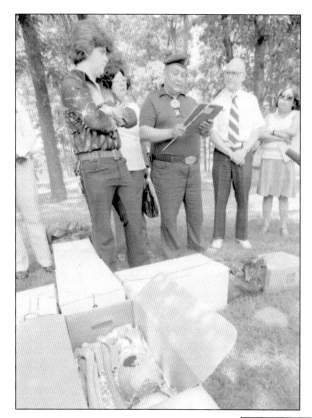

When white Europeans started navigating southeastern Michigan following the fur trade, they found major tribes inhabiting the land, including the Ojibwe and Chippewas. Indian trails crisscrossed the land and evidence of agricultural cultivation was found by early settlers in the area of South Rochester in the Clinton River Valley. As the area developed, burial grounds and remains were often disturbed. (Courtesy of Walter P. Reuther Library.)

Today there are federal regulations such as the Native American Graves Protection and Repatriation Act to help protect gravesites. The act passed in 1990 and requires federal agencies and institutions that receive federal funding to return Native American cultural items and human remains to their respective peoples. (Courtesy of Walter P. Reuther Library.)

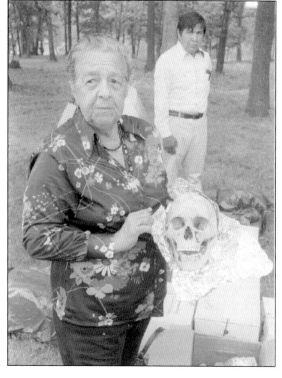

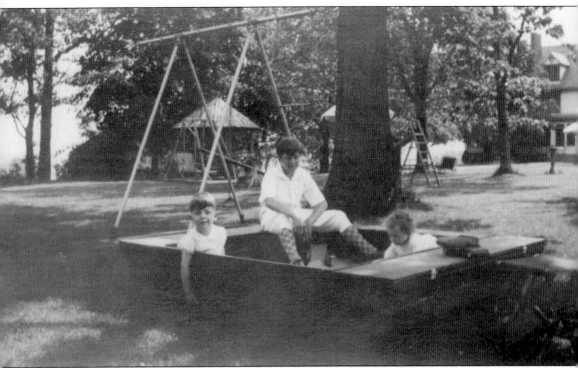

Daniel Dodge looks over his younger brother, Richard Wilson, in a sandbox on the farm property. The family has many stories of the trouble Danny and his Wilson cousins down the street would get into while Meadow Brook Farm was being built. It turns out wooden scaffolds made a great jungle gym for young boys! Alfred Wilson's brother Don Wilson lived farther south down Adams Road from Meadow Brook Farms, in the house used by the Presbyterian Church today. (Courtesy of Meadow Brook Hall.)

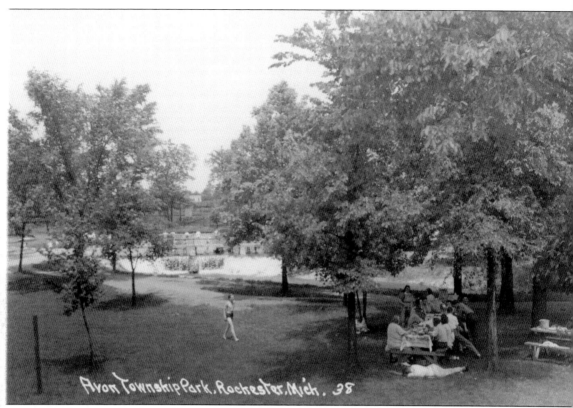

Now known as Rochester Municipal Park, Avon Township Park has been a community gathering spot since 1933. The federal government's Public Works Administration provided labor and the township provided materials and land to develop a public park on John C. Day's farmland along Paint Creek.

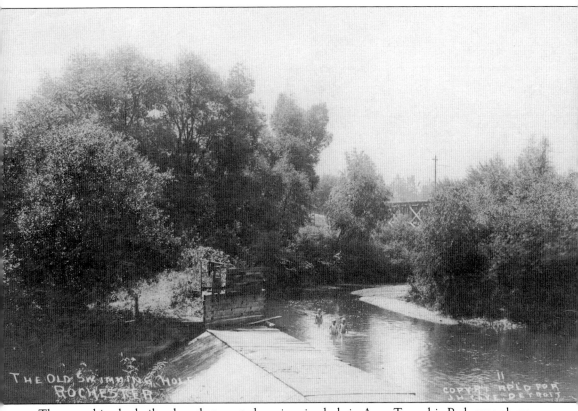

The township also built a dam that created a swimming hole in Avon Township Park, seen above. Now 25 acres, the park boasts several playgrounds, tennis and volleyball courts, pavilions, and a community house. Through the park runs Paint Creek Trail, a bike path from Rochester to Lake Orion that follows the old rail beds of the 1872 Detroit and Bay City Railroad. The municipal park hosts the Arts & Apples festival every autumn.

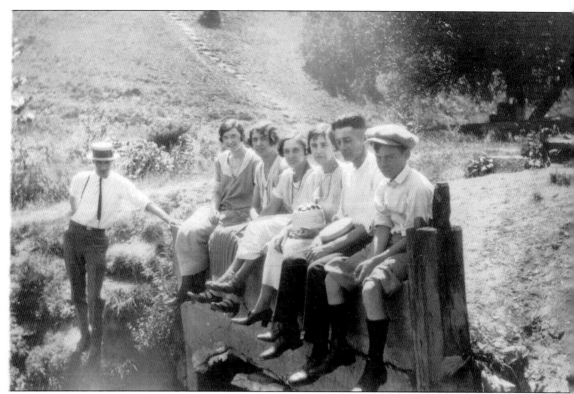

After John and Horace Dodge passed in 1920, Howard Bradley Bloomer, chairman of the Dodge Brothers Motor Car Company, convinced the board to donate some Dodge company land to the state to create public parks to memorialize the brothers. This type of recreation kept with the Dodge family's love of the outdoors. The board quickly set aside nearly 700 acres upon which several parks were created around Metro Detroit.

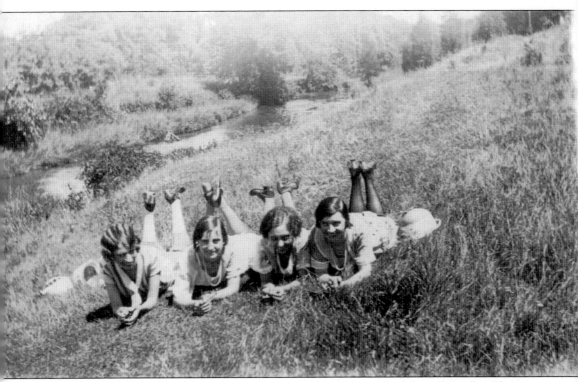

When the Dodge Brothers Motor Company donated land for parks, Howard Bradley Bloomer decided to donate some land as well. One in particular, park No. 2, was in close proximity to Rochester. As these four women understand, the Oakland County Highway catalog from 1924 states, "And from the hill-tops one can breathe the clean air of open country and look into the secrets of pretty valleys all about."

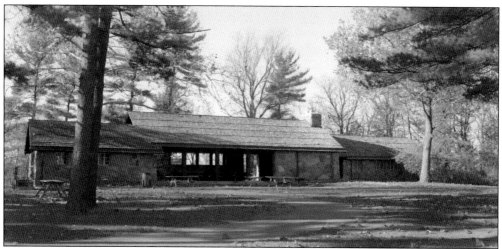

As part of New Deal legislation of the Great Depression, the federal government had the Civilian Conservation Corps landscape Bloomer Park and build this beautiful stone picnic pavilion. For the nearly 25 percent of the American population that was unemployed, federal programs such as these not only gave people hope they would survive but also created beautiful spaces in towns across the nation.

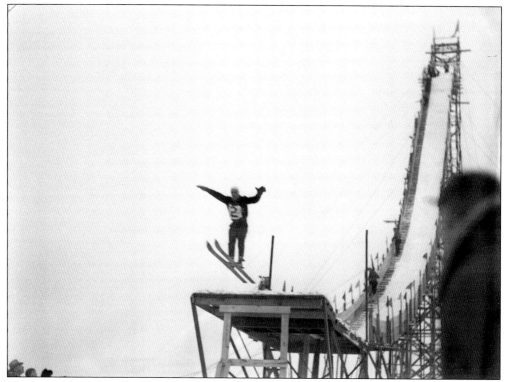

The late 19th and early 20th centuries saw a vast increase in Americans' desires for recreation, and skiing exploded in popularity. It had existed in various forms for thousands of years, but it was Sondre Norheim in 1850 who invented the perfect heel strap that enabled modern downhill and ski jumping. In 1926, the Hall brothers of Detroit built the largest ski jump in the Lower Peninsula in Rochester's Bloomer Park. (Courtesy of Walter P. Reuther Library.)

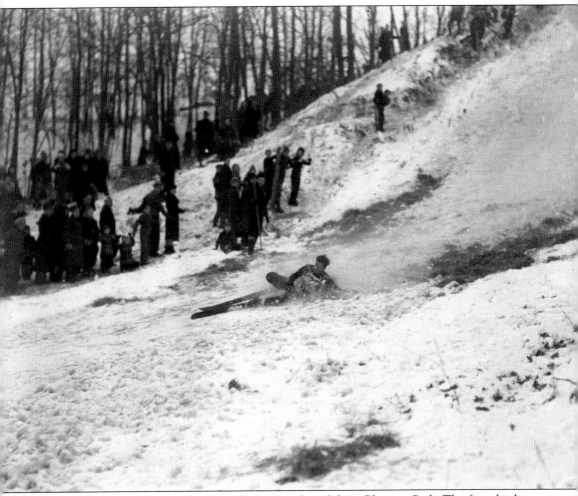

Rochester was quite progressive to build this 112-foot slide in Bloomer Park. The first ski shop in the United States had just opened in a much larger city, Boston, the same year. The Red Wing Ski Club was started by a local group of boys who were in the Detroit Ski Club, and they joined international competitions using this slide to host their own. The slide was also open to local residents. Unfortunately, the jump did not have longevity. Despite garnering national and international recognition, Mother Nature had other plans. A large windstorm hit the area and destroyed the slide in 1934 then again in 1940, a few years later after it was rebuilt. This photograph predates the second collapse by a year, showing the dangers even an experienced skier faced surmounting the jump. (Courtesy of Walter P. Reuther Library.)

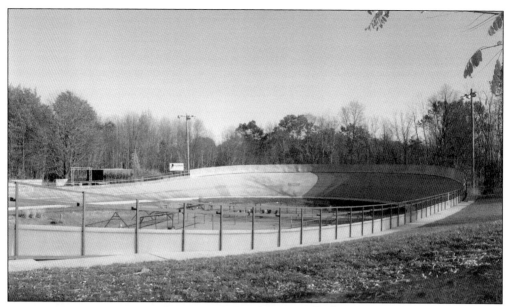

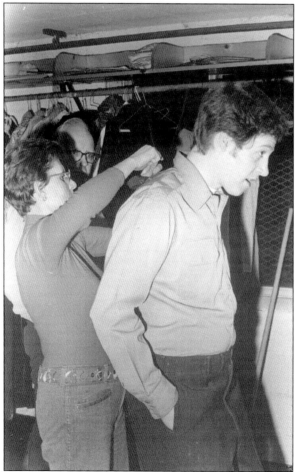

Built in 2001 with a crew of volunteers, the Bloomer Park Velodrome was born. Drafted by Olympic velodrome designer Dale Hughes, all monies for the project were raised independently of the city and its maintenance is continually funded through the generosity of the Mike Walden Velodrome Fund and the Community Foundation. This is one of less than two dozen tracks in the country for outdoor riding.

Many of the volunteers of the Avon Players have been members and supporters for decades. Tim Lentz and makeup artist Joyce Harner, preparing for the 1975–1976 production of *Subject Was Roses*, are examples of this trend. Administration manager Marlaina Jurco describes the members as a close-knit family. Entirely operated by volunteers, the group's survival attests to the selflessness and creativity of Rochester, as well as the supportive cultural community. (Courtesy of Avon Players.)

The Avon Players began with the desire of a church theater group to share its talents with the community. In 1947, it began performing at the old Rochester High School. Then in 1965, Sarah Van Hoosen donated property, which sits adjacent to the old village of Stoney Creek, and a unique A-frame was built in its current location. This interior shot represents the difficulties in creating a stage set, particularly as the nature of theater changed and more dynamic, revolving sets came into vogue. The pitched roof and low sloping sides demand the set designers think creatively. In 2001, the Avon Players built an incredible two-story set for *A Streetcar Named Desire*, proving the group's creativity. (Photographs by Britt Photographic; courtesy of Avon Players.)

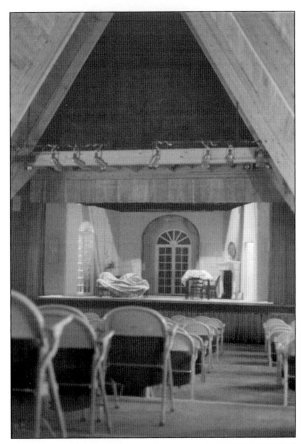

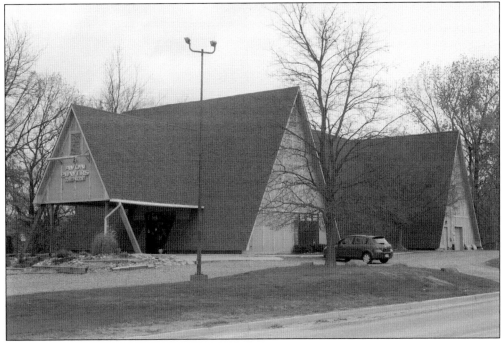

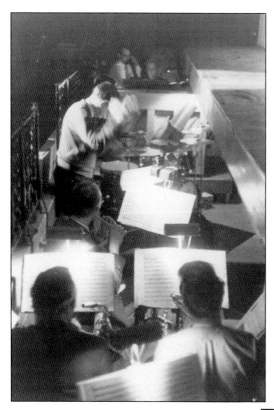

The actors, administrators, set and costume designers, and crew of the Avon Players are volunteers, but as the photograph below shows, the end results are far from lacking. One can imagine the audience leaning forward in anticipation of what the actors will say next. The undated photograph of the orchestra pit at left conveys the passion an orchestra adds to a performance. The strong shadows and diagonal lines dividing the picture lend an almost secretive air to its presence. Hidden below the stage, the orchestra's climactic crescendos and foreboding staccatos resonate with the audience. (Courtesy of Avon Players.)

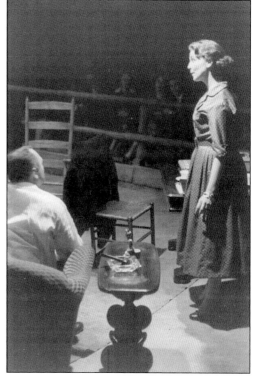

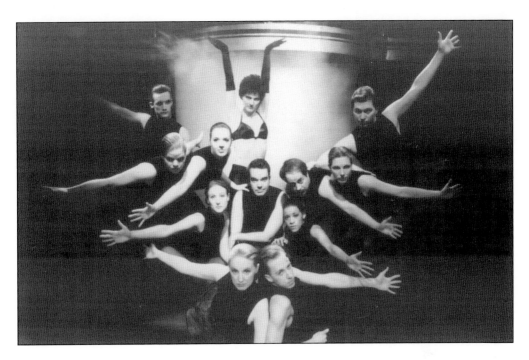

The 1990s saw fantastic performances by the Avon Players. In 1995, *Chicago* proved that the aspirations and artistic endeavors of the members have matured since church friends started the group 50 years earlier. This photograph is professional and magnetic, showing how far the Avon Players have come. The set of *The Secret Garden* (below) is held with much pride within the group. The elaborate topiaries give the illusion the audience is inside the walled confines of the garden. (Photographs by Britt Photographic; courtesy of Avon Players.)

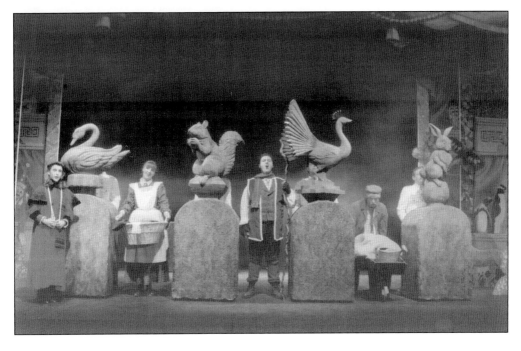

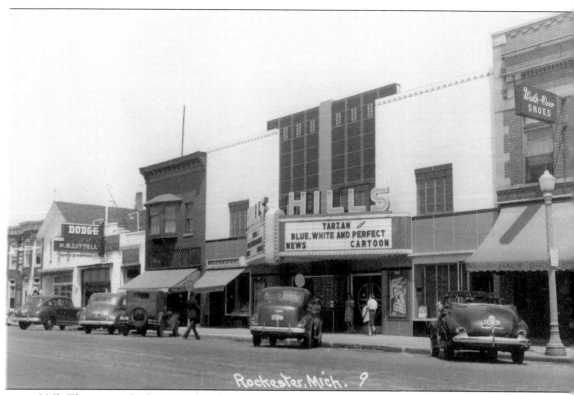

Hills Theater was built in 1941 by Charles L. Stearns, the owner of Rochester's other movie house, Avon Theater. This very Moderne-style theater was faced with Vitrolite, a glass tile that made the lines and surface of this geometric building especially stunning. In 1943, when *Tarzan* and *Blue, White, and Perfect* were released, the movie theater held a special meaning for residents: it was the place to see current newsreels about the soldiers and action in World War II. At a time when radios and newspapers delivered the news, these films were especially poignant as they allowed Americans to imagine it was their brothers, their sons, their fathers, and their husbands who were marching down streets or arriving safely back at camp. Notice the marquee advertises news and cartoons. Children (and adults) loved watching the animated shorts that appeared after the movie. In 1985, Hills Theater finally bowed to the giant theaters that had siphoned away its customers.

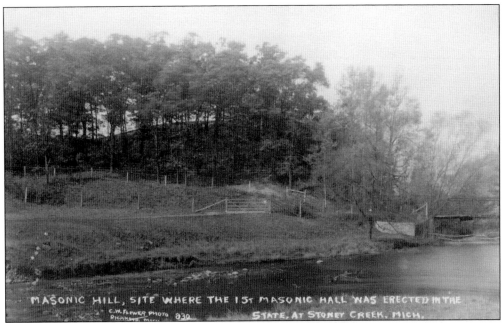

The first Masonic Temple built in Michigan was at Mount Morriah in Stoney Creek. Built in 1847 by Stoney Creek Lodge No. 5, the wood framed building was painted red and stood on a tall foundation. A single door was added. The members walked through the cellar to reach a staircase that ascended to the lodge room. Although the structure is gone, one can still see the hill on which the temple originally stood.

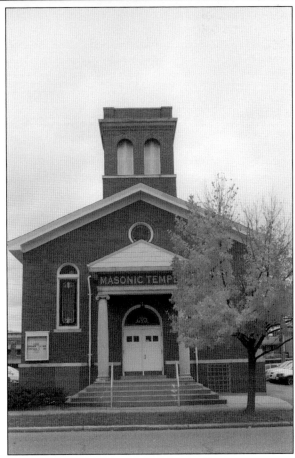

The local Masonic chapter originally met in the 19th-century structure on Main Street, but in 1959 it moved into this 1867 building. Masons are a long-standing fraternal organization dedicated to philanthropic ideals that better mankind through charitable acts, often with no recognition for individuals. Most of the original settlers in Stoney Creek were Masons. (Photographed by the authors.)

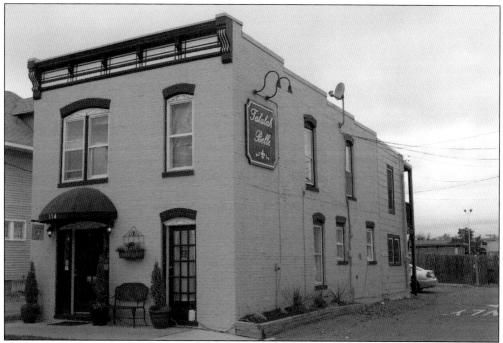

This brick, two-story building still stands at 114 West Third Street. Originally home to the *Rochester Era* newspaper, it was built around 1873 by Truman Buell Fox and his wife, Sarah, who moved to Rochester to start the small paper. After Truman passed in 1893, his son William took over the day-to-day operations. In 1949 it was sold to the Rochester *Clarion*.

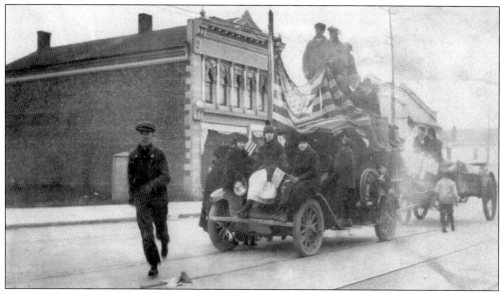

Cries of joy were heard around the world on November 11, 1918, Armistice Day, when the Allies and the Germans agreed to stop hostilities and negotiate an end to World War I. It was referred to as the "war to end all wars," and many spontaneous and planned celebrations erupted across the nation when news of peace was delivered. Such celebrations are seen here in downtown Rochester.

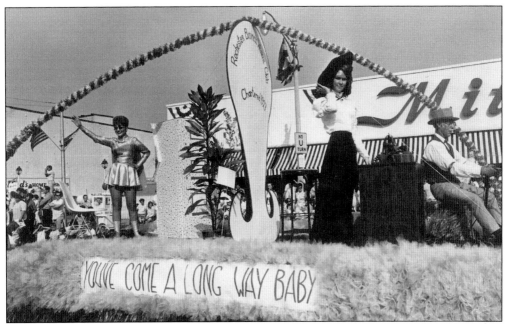

The Rochester Business Women's Club was established in 1927 and has been instrumental in the community, donating money to scholarship funds at Oakland University as well as high schools. This float appears to show a suffragette and a woman of the future, playing on the featured proclamation that women have "come a long way." (Courtesy of Rochester Hills Museum.)

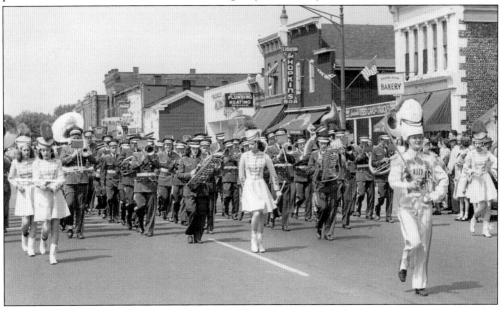

The 20th century saw developments in child psychology and the importance of supporting the maturation and education of youth. Although the concepts of child education have gone through changes, it is still maintained that art and music are an indispensable part of a child's development. This high school marching band marches down Main Street in front of the Old Stone Store. Notice the used car lot to its right, where Red Knapp's Dairy Bar is now. (Courtesy of Rochester Hills Museum.)

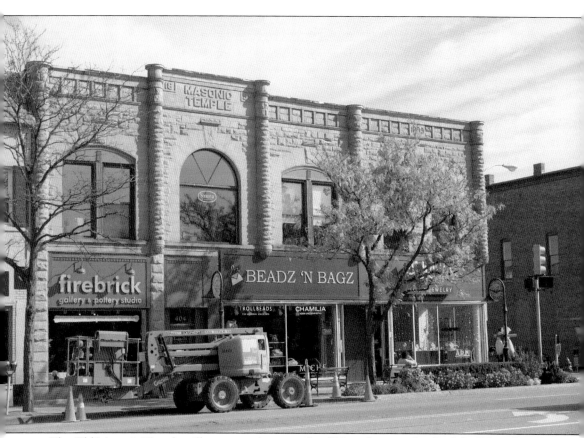

The Old Masonic Temple still exists on the east side of Main Street today. Built by Edward Prall at the turn of the century to house the Masons, it has hosted several other businesses, including the town jail. This modern image shows a "cherry-picker" on the sidewalk, preparing for one of Rochester's biggest draws, the Big Bright Light Show. A tradition since 2006, buildings are strung with lights from top to bottom, giving the Main Street corridor a color block print that never fails to get people in the holiday spirit. Though Rochester's Christmas light show and parade is now a spectacle of technology and commerce, it had rather more humble beginnings, once featuring a parade and Christmas tree. Meadow Brook Hall also draws crowds for its annual holiday walk, started in 1971. Each room is decorated differently, and some 10,000 visitors attend to see the hall in its holiday splendor.

BIBLIOGRAPHY

Eisenberg, William D. *Leading the Way: The Story of Leader Dogs for the Blind.* Rochester: Gold Leaf Press, 2008.
Farris, Anne. *Historical Tour Guide: A Walking and Driving Tour to Rochester, Rochester Hills, and Stoney Creek Michigan.* Rochester: Rochester-Avon Historical Society, 1998.
Fey, Charles. *History of Freemasonry in Oakland County, Michigan.* Self-published, 1949.
Fox, W.A. *Beautiful Rochester.* Rochester: Avon Printing Company, 1990.
———. *Rochester: A Sketch of One of the Best Towns on the Map.* Self-published, 1907.
Gibbs, Margaret. *Leader Dogs for the Blind.* Fairfax, VA: Delinger's Publisher, 1982.
Hill, Karen. "Mr. McGregor's Garden." *Oakland University Magazine* (Winter 1989) 6–9.
Jurco, Marlaina. Interview by authors. Rochester Hills, September 22, 2010.
McAlester, Virginia and Lee. *A Field Guide to American Houses.* New York: Alfred A. Knopf, 1994.
Pray, Eula. *A History of Avon Township: 1820–1940.* Ann Arbor, MI: The Nonce Press, 1986.
Rochester-Avon Historical Society. *Historical Tour of the City of Rochester and Avon Township.* Rochester: Rochester-Avon Historical Society, 1980.
———. *Rochester: Preserving History, A Pictorial Journey.* Rochester: Rochester-Avon Historical Society, 2000.
Rochester Centennial Commission. *"A Lively Town:" 152 Years in Rochester.* Rochester: Rochester Centennial Commission Inc., 1969.
Rochester Historical Commission. *Dateline: Rochester: Headlines from Rochester's History.* Rochester: Rochester Historical Commission, 1990.
Seeley, Thaddeus De Witt. *History of Oakland County, Michigan, Volume 1.* Chicago: The Lewis Publishing Company, 1912.
Smith, Katharine P. "Rochester Hills Woman Recalls Walter P. Reuther." *Detroit Free Press,* August 3, 2008.
Snook, Arthur. Interview by author. Rochester, September 2010.
Stewart, Larry. *The Seasons of Rochester College.* Rochester: Rochester College, 2008.
Van Hoosen, Bertha. *Petticoat Surgeon.* New York: Arno Press Inc., 1980.
Williams, Dan. Interview by author. Rochester, July 2010.
Williams, Robert. "80 Years with Michigan Angus." *Michigan Angus* (March 1963) 1–24.

Discover Thousands of Local History Books Featuring Millions of Vintage Images

Arcadia Publishing, the leading local history publisher in the United States, is committed to making history accessible and meaningful through publishing books that celebrate and preserve the heritage of America's people and places.

Find more books like this at
www.arcadiapublishing.com

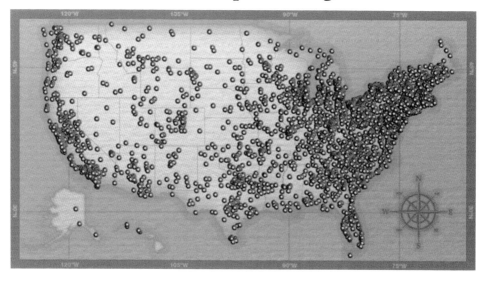

Search for your hometown history, your old stomping grounds, and even your favorite sports team.

Consistent with our mission to preserve history on a local level, this book was printed in South Carolina on American-made paper and manufactured entirely in the United States. Products carrying the accredited Forest Stewardship Council (FSC) label are printed on 100 percent FSC-certified paper.

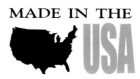